November 2001

It is good to be able to
share Jon Walton's sermons
with you, Chuck!
God be with you,
Marilyn

Imperfect Peace

*Other Titles in the
Teaching Sermon Series*

THE TEACHING SERMON SERIES

Ronald J. Allen, Editor

Imperfect Peace

Teaching Sermons on Troubling Texts

JON M. WALTON

Abingdon Press
Nashville

IMPERFECT PEACE
TEACHING SERMONS ON TROUBLING TEXTS

Copyright © 1999 by Abingdon Press

This book is printed on acid-free paper.

Library of Congress Cataloging-in-Publication Data

Walton, Jon M., 1947-
    Imperfect peace : teaching sermons on troubling texts / Jon. M. Walton.
        p. cm. — (The teaching sermon series)
    Includes bibliographical references.
    ISBN 0-687-06014-1 (pbk. : alk. paper)
    1. Bible—Sermons. 2. Teaching sermons. 3. Sermons, American.
I. Title. II. Series.
BS491.5.W36   1999
252—dc21   98-48116
                                                                        CIP

Scripture quotations, unless otherwise noted, are from the New Revised Standard Version of the Bible. Copyright © 1989 by the Division of Christian Education of the National Council of the Churches of Christ in the United States of America. All rights reserved.

Those noted KJV are from the King James Version of the Bible.

Those noted NKJV are from the New King James Version. Copyright © 1979, 1980, 1982, Thomas Nelson Inc., Publishers.

"The Great Flood," from *Noah's Ark* by Peter Spier. Translation copyright © 1977 by Peter Spier. Used by permission of Doubleday, a division of Bantam Doubleday Dell Publishing Group, Inc., and William Heinemann, a division of Egmont Children's Books Ltd.

00 01 02 03 04 05 06 07 08 —10 9 8 7 6 5 4 3 2

MANUFACTURED IN THE UNITED STATES OF AMERICA

In memory of

Edmund Steimle

Preacher, Teacher, and Friend

Contents

A FEW YEARS AGO I WAS SERVING A CONGREGATION ON Long Island, a picturesque Currier & Ives kind of church on a village green, with over three hundred years of history. The congregation was a mixture of shopkeepers, business-men and businesswomen, New York commuters, a number of elementary schoolteachers, and faculty members from a nearby state university. They were articulate about their faith and their doubts.

One Sunday morning, I rose before the congregation to read the lectionary assignment for the day—Mark 10:2-16, a controversial story in which Jesus discusses the problem of divorce with the Pharisees. Part of the text carries the shock-ing admonition that "whoever divorces his wife and marries another commits adultery against her; and if she divorces her husband and marries another, she commits adultery."

That Sunday, a member of the congregation heard these words as if for the first time. Jim was divorced and remar-ried, as was his wife, and he was not about to be told that he or his spouse were adulterers! He never heard a word of my sermon, but rather sat through the remainder of the service building up a head of steam. By Sunday afternoon, having had some time to simmer down, he fired off a letter to me, mincing no words: "How dare you stand in the pulpit and read a passage like that?"

With utter clarity, Jim, out of his own experience, identi-fied his disagreement with the text. It sounded to Jim as if his own experience of grace and forgiveness as a remarried divorcé in the church was being denied by a text that rang down condemnation on him. It was a judgment that he viewed as patently unfair and unworthy of the fullness of the gospel. It took several discussions with Jim to ease his discomfort with the text. We talked about the situation the passage was addressing, and the purpose of this saying in light of the view of the law expressed in Mark's Gospel. Eventually Jim came to a relationship with the passage that seemed true to his best instincts about God and life. In the process, I learned from him that I had at least one parishioner who was listening closely to the Scripture readings in worship and sometimes was disagreeing with them.

There are many texts that leave us wondering how we can reconcile them with our experience of life, our understanding of God, our knowledge of the gospel, and our conviction of the love and grace of God made known in Jesus Christ. Whether a preacher is devoted to the lectionary or selects texts through a "hunt and peck" method, these passages are bound to cause trouble for the soul of the preacher and his or her congregation. In the end, we find we disagree with some of these passages.

Some preachers may say, "What do you mean you disagree with the text? The Word of God is the WORD OF GOD. Our only purpose is to hear and obey it." Of course over the centuries the church has learned that when we gather around the Bible, we often discover the will and word of God. Many of the passages in the Bible inform our faith directly. However, some passages invite our arguments, disagreements, and opposite conclusions. These passages seem to deny the core proclamation that our God is a God of goodness, justice, and love. Unless we can bring that lively exchange to our understanding of the Scriptures, we deny our intellect and emotional responses, and we limit our faith. My experience is that when I disagree with a passage, the process of clarifying my disagreement usually helps me clarify as well what I most truly believe about God.

There are many such texts raising important theological issues with which Christians have struggled for centuries. Others lie at the heart of the church's struggle with current issues of social justice: inclusive language; women's concerns; welcoming gay men and lesbians in church membership and ordination; relationships between Christianity and Judaism; and other issues of theological import. When we disagree with a text, we come to a teachable moment, an intersection between faith, doubt, and curiosity; and there our faith may deepen.

A Methodology for Problematic Texts

When preaching on a problematic text, a text with which you find you have a disagreement, a number of issues must be addressed, starting with a naive reading of the passage. I suggest that the preacher read the text several times and do so as the most uninformed of readers might encounter it. Lay aside all theological sophistication and ask how a non-believer, a nine-year-old, or a person new to faith might hear this passage. Take the text literally. What is it asking you to do or believe? Jesus says, for instance, that "if your right hand causes you to sin, cut it off and throw it away" (Matt. 5:30). But should you really cut off your right hand? Who in their right mind would do such a thing? And if the body is the temple of God, isn't such defilement another form of sin?

Write down all of the questions this text raises for you without attempting to resolve the contradictions or the offensiveness of its witness. Many in the congregation will hear the text similarly. Unless some of these questions and problems are acknowledged in the sermon, the congregation will take them home unresolved. The naive questions also help you to hear the text afresh, stripped of the many things you already know and the things you are aware you do not know about what this passage is saying.

Can you find any complementary or antithetical passages of Scripture that amplify or contradict the text? For instance, the body is the temple of God, so wouldn't cutting off my sinful right hand in order to gain heaven be a severe approach to resolving a moral dilemma?

Some of the disagreement we have with a text comes from a knowledge of the fact that other scriptures may have other things to say to the issue. We will want to ask what do physical sciences, social sciences, philosophy, core teachings of Christian doctrine, other religious traditions, and even common sense have to say to the text. For example, if the passage under scrutiny is one of the Genesis creation accounts (Gen. 1:1; Gen. 2:4), the preacher must take into account the scientific accounts of the creation that take a different point of view from the biblical versions.

Now that you have some initial reactions to the text, you will need to hear it on its own terms and in its own context. This is the work of exegesis. Word study; contextual location in the gospel; similar and dissimilar themes and situations in the same book and elsewhere in the Scriptures; close reading of the commentaries—all give clues and signs to explore. What do you know of the biblical writer's use of language; his or her editing purposes, theological biases; the community being addressed? Are these preexilic or postexilic prophetic concerns? Is this passage's literary genre narrative, myth, fable, poetry, holiness code, controversy story, a healing account, or eschatology? When we are able to answer these questions we are often able to know why a text was formulated in its specific way in its ancient context. We can understand, for instance, why Mark's account of the prohibition against divorce was so stringent, or why Matthew's edition of the gospel teaches that we should cut off our hand if it causes us to sin. How has it been understood in its various historical contexts? How might it have been heard in the community for whose sake it was first written and recorded?

Can you state clearly what is the problem you are having with this passage? In order to articulate your disagreement, you need to know exactly what it is that is troubling you about the claim the text makes upon you. Knowing those questions may lead us to ask others, which will drive you deeper into the meaning within the text and the issues of faith that the text is leading you to explore. Is it the first-century, non-scientific viewpoint that is your point of departure, the depiction of a God who creates the universe without benefit of a Big Bang? Is there anything still to be gained or learned from a faith that knows God in that way?

Are you rejecting the idea of a cruel and vengeful God who orders the destruction of Jericho and the slaughter of its inhabitants—"men and women, young and old, oxen, sheep, and donkeys" (Josh. 6:21)—or even worse, the destruction of the entire earth through a flood? Is God always and only a peacemaker, or can we imagine that God gets angry, too? If God gets angry as humans do, then what is the true nature of this God we worship?

Do you disagree with the portrayal of a God who seems too capricious, like a landowner who hires laborers at varying times of the day and pays them all the same wage (Matt. 20:1-16)? Or, is God too judgmental and harsh, like the owner of the house who stands behind a shut door that he will not open to the supplicant (Luke 13:23-27)? Knowing exactly what it is in the passage that seems out of synch with contemporary life, even our own biases and prejudices, will help clarify how we address and respond to its message. In some cases you may find that your own faith needs to be instructed by the corrective, balancing word the text bears. In other cases your ability to pinpoint and articulate your disagreements with the text will demonstrate for the congregation both how to think theologically and how to address their own questions and disagreements with Scripture. Without that clarity, the congregation may not know where the preacher's doubts end and faith begins, and some may leave worship wondering whether their pastor believes anything at all in the Bible.

The preacher functions as a guide in that respect, demon-

strating that a "thinking Christian" is not an oxymoron. In
that vein, one of the kindest responses a preacher may hear
at the door after worship are the words, "Thanks for struggling with that passage this morning. You've helped me
understand it better."

On many occasions I have found myself arguing with a
text, thinking that I strongly disagreed with it, only to find
after further study that I had misunderstood what it had to
say. I had not read it carefully, or had heard only part of its
message. At times I find that I continue to disagree with a
part of the text, but discover ironically that I agree with
another part of the same passage. In the sermon "The
Flood," for instance, I began study of the text believing that I
had a fundamental disagreement with a story of a God of
vengeance who would send a natural disaster to punish the
Creation for sin. Surely God would not destroy people, land,
and all living things like that! But closer reading showed me
there are elements of the story that are fundamental to faith
and indivisible from the entire story. This caused me to
rethink my original assumptions and move from resistance
to receptivity, acknowledging that while I continued to disagree with some aspects of how God is represented in the
story, there were at the same time other aspects that are
essential to faith and cannot be denied. The Scriptures
encounter, challenge, and teach us in unexpected ways.

In the end, we may argue with the text, disagree with it,
rail against it, praise it, or wonder at it, but we cannot
ignore it. We must, instead, allow the text to be a light from
which all our questions and scholarship draw illumination.
It is to the text, then, that we must always return in our
study so that God may speak to us from our encounter with
it. In its light our questions and disagreements become the
means by which we can come to better understand not only
the text but also ourselves, and most importantly the God
who is the end of all our seeking.

Chapter One

Divorce

The undeniably clear answer Jesus gives the Pharisees who question him in Matthew 5:31-32 and 19:3-9 about the conditions under which divorce is permissible seems uncharacteristically harsh coming from one so full of compassion. In a society in which almost half of all marriages end in divorce, we have to ask how we can live up to such an unbending measure of morality. Like my parishioner Jim, who heard the Markan version of this saying read in worship and rejected it as something Jesus could never have said, I wonder how I can preach this text with compassion for those who have struggled with marriage and found they could not go on. Certainly quoting Jesus' words, "whoever divorces his wife . . . and marries another commits adultery," provides little in the way of pastoral understanding for complicated human dilemmas. Most of those I have counselled who are going through divorce are wrestling with a heavy burden of guilt, feelings of failure and self-doubt, and questions of whether they are able to keep commitments.

Divorce is a complex matter, every bit as complex as marriage itself. Some people never seem to forgive themselves for the marriage that they couldn't make work. A few divorce freely and easily at the first sign that things are not working out. Some live lives of pain and anguish, grieving a love that has grown cold, while attempting slavishly to fulfill a vow of fidelity in marriage, yet having been emotionally abandoned by a partner who is no longer the person he or she once was. How does a preacher address all the conditions of need within a congregation in which each of these listeners may be present?

In the sermon that follows, I have opted to address the situation of the person within the faith community who has sincerely wrestled with the challenges of divorce and isn't sure what to make of the apparent condemnation in Jesus' words. The task is to discern Jesus' meaning and purpose within his historical context, to remain faithful to it in the hermeneutical work of transferring the meaning of the message to today, and weighing all of this on the scale of a gospel in which the love of God exceeds the collective sin in any and all of us.

Whoever Divorces

Matthew 5:31-32; 19:3-9

NOBODY COULD POSSIBLY like divorce. That's not to say that, looking back on your life, it may not have been the best thing you could have done for your emotional health—to separate from someone who did not love you, someone who was physically or verbally abusive or whose drinking destroyed all you had together.

I doubt that there are many who stand before a minister at a wedding who do so "lightly or unadvisedly," as the familiar words of the old marriage ceremony admonish. The vast majority, if not all, are sincere in their desire to keep the promises they make, to love that other person "for better, for worse; for richer, for poorer; in sickness and in health; to love and to cherish, till death us do part." Marriage, unlike a lot of other things in life, is intended to last a lifetime.

When my sister and brother-in-law were working their way through their divorce, my nephew said to his mother, "When I get married it will be forever." And my sister's only thought was, "But when your dad and I got married it was for the rest of our lives, too."

Unfortunately, divorce has touched nearly every family in America in one way or another. If you yourself have not been divorced, then most likely someone in your family has. Divorce ends half of all marriages in our country. Statistics indicate that those who remarry after divorce are more likely to divorce again than those who marry for the first time. What is it that makes us have such unstable marriages these days, and why do so many end in divorce?

There are, I think, as many reasons why marriages fail or succeed as there are marriages. Not all of us go through the same stresses or face the same crises, and we are not all the same people. We bring differing personalities and temperaments to working through the challenges of life together. Some couples face very few problems but just can't seem to make it, while others face enormous complications which only draw them closer. And how do you explain that?

> *Some couples face very few problems but just can't seem to make it, while others face enormous complications which only draw them closer. And how do you explain that?*

I don't think it's possible to make a complete list of the reasons why marriages fail. You know the reasons as well as I do. Infidelity, boredom, bickering . . . : Things happen; people change—but not always together. A child dies, and the stresses and the blaming tear the marriage apart. The failure to find common values drives a wedge between two people who thought they had so much in common. Youthfulness and immaturity sometimes figure into the equation; he wants to go out with the boys drinking, while she is expected to stay home each evening and watch romantic movies on TV. Or, there may be mental or physical abuse—shouting, arguing, or the inability to settle disagreements peaceably and constructively. There are as many reasons why marriages fail as there are marriages that fail.

Maybe if we understood why people get married we might understand a little more of why they divorce. In the time of Jesus, people married for different reasons than people marry today. They married first of all by arrangement. The father of the bride made an agreement with the father of the groom, a contract that might be made when the bride was eight or nine years old, a promise that when she reached puberty she might be given to the man as his wife. A dowry was arranged, a bride payment, and the contract was struck. If you were wealthy, perhaps your marriage might be arranged to enhance your fortune, or to further a political alliance, or to improve your social standing. Maybe you would be in love with your spouse; maybe not. Love and happiness was not the point; that was secondary. Of more importance in marriage was obedience, progeny, inheritance, and land. Everyone understood that.

Divorce was not unheard of even in the Old Testament. The book of Deuteronomy makes allowance for divorce (Deut. 24:1), but its justice is weighted in favor of men. Just give your wife a certificate and tell her it's over. Send her out for cigarettes, and change the locks! It was virtually that simple. Which is why, centuries later, Jesus was so appalled by it and sought to change it.

Today, people get married more often than not for love. And as Shakespeare, Leo Buscaglia, and St. Paul have all made abundantly clear: love is not only a many splendored thing, but also a very complicated thing. People get married because they love each other to pieces, yes. But they also get married—sometimes knowingly, sometimes unknowingly— because they are bored and find someone witty, or because they are poor and find someone rich, or because they think very poorly of themselves and find someone who thinks well of them and whom they believe may be their only hope of marriage. Some people marry the very image of their father or of their mother, and want their spouse to treat them that way. Some in widowhood or older age find someone to be a companion and friend, and do not wish more than that. Some marry an image of the person they think they see and know, but which is not the reality at all. We marry because life is difficult and lonely, and it feels better to have someone with whom to walk than it does to walk alone. We marry for love, yes, and yet for many complicated reasons.

I think about that sometimes, how complicated marriage is, as I look in the eyes of two star-crossed lovers as they stand before me on their wedding day and make solemn promises of love and faithfulness to each other. Once or twice I have been asked to preach or to offer some advice within the wedding ceremony to a couple being married. Not long ago I found myself saying to a couple these words:

> You will probably never do anything quite so brash, quite so brave, or quite so important again in your whole life as you are doing now.
>
> Marriage is an adventure. It is starting off on a journey . . . which only you can traverse as your experience. You will come at times to high trails that will demand your all, taking you above tree line where you may feel lonely and lost. At other times you will find yourself in hot, arid places feeling parched and weary, not sure you want to go on. You will come to verdant glens and beautiful gardens where you may give your bodies to the sun and breathe the clean air and smell the beautiful flowers. . . . At times you will hold hands and lie together and be at peace. And at other times you may need to walk apart, perhaps one leading the way, and then the other. But never lose sight of each other. Never get so far ahead or stay so far behind that you cannot be a help, a friend, a lover, a companion along the way. Because of what you have decided today, your character and identity are now determinatively linked to this other; you are companions on this journey from now on.

It's idealized, yes, and I'm not sure the couple I was marrying got even half of what I said. I'm not sure any couple really *gets it* all that much standing glassy-eyed and excited, romantic and breathless at the altar. None of us can possibly have any idea what will lie ahead of us, what we will have to face in life, what stresses and gauntlets we will have to endure. And if we did, perhaps fewer people might be so anxious to go ahead and get married. But then maybe some might be brave enough to go ahead after all.

Some of the most important things we have to learn in marriage are not anything anybody can teach you anyway, but things we can only learn by experiencing them and doing the best we can with them. And some come to their seventy-fifth wedding anniversary, full of wrinkles and love—still together. And some quite literally never make it much past the starting gate. Heaven only knows why.

The Pharisees came to Jesus once and asked if he knew any good reason for getting a divorce. It was a trick question probably, like many questions the Pharisees asked him. If he had said there wasn't any good reason for divorce, then he would have angered his Jewish followers who appreciated the ease with which a divorce might be obtained (just write a certificate and wash your hands). Likewise the Gentiles of Matthew's church, overhearing this story, would have thought Jesus was hopelessly out of touch with reality if he had said there were no grounds for divorce at all. So Jesus answered the Pharisees with a reference to the Torah story in which God creates man and woman, male and female, and gives them to each other to become one flesh, making one life together. We ought to be like that, Jesus seemed to say.

"Well, if we ought to be like that, then how come Moses said it was all right to divorce?" retorted the Pharisees. And Jesus answered, "Because you are so hard-hearted." And then comes that hard-to-hear phrase: "Whoever divorces his wife, except for unchastity, and marries another commits adultery."

Now at surface level this would sound like an incredibly sexist and legalistic approach to the heartbreaking reality of divorce, an uncharacteristically cold and indifferent answer from Jesus, who is not normally so brusque.

And yet one Jewish scholar, Phillip Sigal, has offered an interesting suggestion about this teaching.[1] He says that Jesus, in this saying, is remarkably protective of women and raises their status dramatically. He does this in three ways. First, Jesus rules against polygamy, saying a man is bound to his first wife even if he divorces her. Second, Jesus removes the double standard by saying that a man is likewise an adulterer if he has a sexual relationship with a second woman. And third, Jesus' strict interpretation of the Deuteronomy passage permitting divorce protects women from the arbitrary power their husbands had to divorce them at will.

That's an interesting new twist on the lemon! But nowadays women are as quick to seek divorce as men, and many a man will tell you that he has been left high and dry in the same way that women in Jesus' day were divorced so freely. No, Jesus' strict teaching still leaves us wondering what to do about the miserable marriage that is hell on earth for all involved, when adultery is not the issue. There are many such folks who have eked out a miserable life together, earning lots of points for perseverance but goose eggs for fulfillment. Jesus does not let up on the issue of divorce, and frankly I see no other way to interpret his words than exactly as we hear them.

So, if the Pharisees were to ask Jesus today, rather than twenty centuries ago, whether or not there may be a just cause for suing for divorce, my guess is that he would say the same thing as he did so long ago, that whoever divorces wife or husband, except on the grounds of unchastity, has violated a sacred covenant. Marriage, in Jesus' mind, was forever. It is entering into a covenant and trying with all your heart not to mess it up.

And yet looking at the scope of Jesus' teachings and the nature of his life and ministry, I think I would also say that there was little about Jesus that was legalistic. He was not one to throw the book at someone, nor to condemn without redemption. There are some passages in the Gospel where the door is shut and judgment rings down without further opportunity for appeal, as in the parable of the wise and foolish maidens in Matthew 25. But for the most part the broad strokes of Jesus' ministry and the great movement of the gospel is into the ocean of love and grace, exemplified by him who gave his life as an example of the extent to which divine love will make sacrifice for our sake.

While I think Jesus would not remove one word from his strict construction of the law that pertains to marriage and divorce, I also think he would be the first of us all to understand the humanity and limitations of each person, the hurts we suffer, sometimes even the hurts we inflict, and surely the promises large and small that we have broken or had to break. I think he would be the first one to urge us to get on with life, to forgive and seek forgiveness, to do the best we can to reconstruct our lives and be at peace.

> *While I think Jesus would not remove one word from his strict construction of the law that pertains to marriage and divorce, I also think he would be the first of us all to understand the humanity and limitations of each person.*

In his encounters with others, with those who had sometimes been hurt in life and by life, Jesus had a way of helping people pick up the pieces and go on. With the woman taken in adultery; with a woman who had been married five times and living with another man; with his own dear friend and disciple Peter, who denied him and whom he restored to fellowship—in each of these encounters, the love and concern of Jesus for the person overrode any other consideration, including their betrayal, failure, or compromised human nature.

I think Jesus would be the first to see that sometimes life's events are such that they just don't work out the way we had hoped, perhaps even the way to which we had committed. Sometimes we just have to accept the limits of our life and do the best we can. Divorce is like that.

Most people do not set out in marriage to end it in divorce. It just happens. Some who have been married a long time and have weathered more than a few storms in their marriage complain that young people nowadays don't hang in there long enough. They say, sure, there have been times when they wanted to leave their spouses, too, but that you just don't *do* that kind of thing. Well, bless you. You have done well—better than many could—in keeping your marriage vows.

But some are going through similar storms in their marriage and find that they cannot go on together. It is too simple to say that it was only a lack of determination, or some kind of moral weakness that makes the difference. Never do we know enough to say that. Maybe all we can do is to be grateful for those who have made it through and found fulfillment on the other side of the stresses of marriage, and try to encourage and stand by and pray *with*, not just *for*, those who have not.

> *Maybe all we can do is to be grateful for those who have made it through and found fulfillment on the other side of the stresses of marriage, and try to encourage and stand by and pray with, not just for, those who have not.*

In his book *The Good News from North Haven* (New York: Doubleday, 1991), Michael Lindvall writes a wonderful story of a marriage under stress. Here he muses on the difficulties and joys of being married.

Life together is hard. There are no perfect husbands, no
perfect wives, no perfect children, no perfect mothers-in-
law. Life in family—life in any community —is both our
sorest test and our sweetest joy. Life together stretches us,
pulls us, strains us, but in it we are nourished by the struggle.

It is the best chance Providence gives most of us to grow
out of ourselves and into something more like what we
were meant to be. . . . For the only thing harder than getting along with other people is getting along without
them. . . .[2]

I wish Jesus had coupled his stern-sounding teaching
about divorce with a milder pastoral tone like that. I know
he had it in him. But maybe he decided that there are times
to say some things and times to keep silent about others.
Times to set up a standard and not complicate it with too
many exceptions. Maybe.

And maybe he said it in that way because marriage is a
covenant and he was comparing it with the covenant God
made with us. God will never break that covenant to be our
God, no matter how bad or wrongheaded or stupid we are.
Maybe it hurt Jesus to see that we do so poorly with our
covenants, that our word does not stand in the same way
God's does. Why else would he say that the only reason for
divorce is because of our hard-heartedness?

> *Sometimes our most solemn promises and our most heart-
> felt commitments cannot be kept. It should not keep us from
> making them. Nor should it keep us from keeping them.*

In any case, knowing Jesus as we do, is there any reason
to believe that divorce is unforgivable? I think not.

In this life we do the best we can. Sometimes our most

solemn promises and our most heartfelt commitments cannot be kept. It should not keep us from making them. Nor should it keep us from keeping them. And somewhere in between we trust that God's love, forgiveness, and care for us is better even than our love, forgiveness, and care for ourselves. In that love we love, and in that forgiveness we forgive and are forgiven.

Chapter Two

Exclusion in the Church

Perhaps one of the most controversial admonitions Paul ever gave the struggling churches of the first century was his advice to the Corinthian men to keep women silent in church. The precise problem within the Corinthian congregation is lost to us, but Paul's counsel is not. The result of that guidance, added to the Jewish customs and traditions out of which Christianity arose, has led to centuries of ambiguity and marginalization for women as leaders in the church. Reason, intellect, experience, and a simple awareness of what is just have shown us that Paul was speaking from a first-century context to a first-century community of believers, which is not the same as the contemporary contexts and communities in which we find ourselves today.

With the move from rural to urban life, suffrage, the education of women, the rise of Western social values, the discussion of feminist issues in a growing number of nations around the world, and the increasing number of Christian denominations that ordain women to sacramental and preaching ministries, the contemporary Christian church finds itself in direct conflict with first-century scriptural authority. Some in the church would argue that this is another example of the loss of "family values," that the church has adopted a secular agenda, and that the ministry and leadership of women weakens the church and weakens the family. I don't agree.

Can we disagree with Scripture and not undercut the very foundations by which it informs and enlightens our faith? Fundamental interpreters of Scripture would say no. But informed and thoughtful people of faith can disagree.

When the Scriptures uphold a position that reason, experience, and intellect cannot support, what are we to do but respectfully dis-

agree? Did God create the universe in seven days? Did a flood cover the entire earth, and were all living things destroyed in that flood save one family and two of every species on earth? Should women keep silent in church? If each of these affirmations are to be taken literally and bear equal weight in truth, then language has utterly failed in its ability to communicate.

We must not ask questions of the Scriptures that the Scriptures are not addressing. Is Genesis prehistoric science? Of course not. The creation accounts of Genesis are witnesses to the faith that God created all things expressed in the language of faith. It is a prescientific testimony to the truth that "in the beginning . . . God" made all things.

Did Paul intend for women never to have a leadership role in the church? Or was Paul addressing a specific question addressed to the issues of one congregation in Corinth? Could Paul have been wrong? Could Paul have been right for his time but not for our time? Can the preacher disagree with Paul, pull on a thread that does not weave well into the fabric without the entire piece unraveling? That is what I attempt to address in this sermon by rephrasing the question of whether women may lead in the church, or whether God's gifts are ever restricted by earthly distinctions. It's an issue that is settled for many Christians in the church and surprisingly unsettled for many others.

Women Should Be Silent in the Churches

> 1 Corinthians 14:34-35;
> 1 Timothy 2:8-15

RECENTLY I WAS ASKED TO preach and teach at a denominational worship and music conference at which I discovered anew that discrimination against women in the church is alive and well in many forms. A woman approached me after one of my classes to tell me about a Mother's Day sermon in her church where the pastor likened men to "hammers—goal-directed, task-oriented"—and women to "thermometers—feeling, reactive." The woman with whom I spoke owns her own real estate business, with earnings in the top 1 percent in the nation, a highly accomplished businessperson in her own right. She told me of the lack of support she received from her pastor in recognizing her gifts as a woman. She said, "My pastor's words made me feel that the Bible has given women a certain place and that God meant for us to stay in it."

Later, after that same class, a group of four women from St. Louis descended on me to tell me about a recent sermon by their pastor in which he admonished all of the women in the congregation who were divorced to go home after the service and get on the telephone and beg forgiveness from their former husbands, asking them for reconciliation. The women asked what I would advise them to do to overcome the oppressive burden of their pastor's views

It was hard for me to believe that such teaching is still being propounded in the church, that anything so alien to the gospel could be offered as a Christian understanding of the role of women. At first I wasn't sure that it could be so. But these women who spoke or wrote to me told of their own experiences, and the witness they bore of discrimination and spiritual abuse was born of the injury and hurt they had suffered at the hands of their pastor.

When the United Presbyterian Church reunited with the Presbyterian Church U.S. only a few years ago, an escape clause permitted an exemption to churches that did not wish to ordain women as elders. We know all too well that the Roman Catholic Church does not permit the ordination of women partially on the basis articulated by church leaders that Jesus did not choose any women to be apostles. In 1994, women meeting at an ecumenical gathering in Minneapolis called the "Reimagining God" conference were roundly criticized for their proposals seeking new and rediscovering ancient images for God found both in Scripture and in the tradition of the church. Discrimination against the gifts, contributions, and concerns of women in the church is alive and well.

> *Discrimination against the gifts, contributions, and concerns of women in the church is alive and well.*

In that vein, the passages from 1 Timothy and from 1 Corinthians advising the church that women should keep silent in the churches ought to sound out of place and inappropriate to our ears these days. But why? Is it simply because these ideas are out of vogue, not modern? That is not enough reason to question them. They are a part of the Bible, so we must contend with what they have to say to us, and understand them on their own terms. Simply not to like the sound of them is not an appropriate reason to reject them.

My concern is twofold. It is to address the question of whether the Bible provides any quarter for discrimination against women, whether in religious settings or elsewhere, and then to look at how we can respond to scriptures that address contemporary problems in terms that give us trouble today. Because unless we find a way to understand women's concerns in the context of our faith, not simply as a secular issue, we will lack a common ground in the church to understand and talk about women's concerns.

Let's start with some biblical perspectives on women. From late Judaism onward, women were prevented from reading Scripture or prophesying. They were relegated to the outer court of the Temple. To this day, in Orthodox Judaism, women sit separately from men and are not permitted to read Scripture or lead in services. This dates to the Levitical codes, which prohibited women from making sacrifices during their monthly menstrual cycle, a condition that would render the sacrifices unclean. Since men might never know when the menstrual cycle would occur, it developed that women never approached the Torah scrolls.

With the coming of Christianity, women began to play a different role within the community of faith. In the early church it was common for women to be teachers. In Paul's Letter to Titus, older women are encouraged to be good teachers of younger women (Titus 2:3-4). In Ephesus, Priscilla instructed Apollos, whose evangelistic zeal was great but whose information about the gospel was lacking (Acts 18:24-26). Paul, in 1 Timothy, urges that women be taught and allowed to learn the faith, a reversal of centuries of Jewish tradition (2:11). Unfortunately, Paul went on to say that women ought to do so in silence. A nifty trick, learning in silence!

In Philippi, two women, Euodia and Syntyche, were co-workers and teachers with Paul and are commended by him as having worked side by side with him (Phil. 4:2-3). Elsewhere, the apostle Philip's four daughters are commended in the book of Acts as prophetesses (21:9), and we know that a wealthy businesswoman, Lydia from Thyatira, a dealer in purple cloth, provided hospitality to Paul and in that sense helped to bankroll Paul's Greater Philippi Crusade (Acts 16:14-15). So women played an important role in the early development of the Christian mission.

As if that weren't enough, Paul, in a pique of revolutionary thinking, wrote to the Galatians that within the Christian community "there is neither Jew nor Greek, there is neither slave nor free, there is neither male nor female; for you are all one in Christ Jesus" (Gal. 3:28 NKJV). Paul was describing the church as a community of people who would love and support one another without regard to worldly distinctions. But in other letters Paul does not demonstrate the same openness toward the equality of women. He teaches, for instance, that women in the bonds of marriage should be subordinate to their husbands, a point the Southern Baptist Convention has recently reaffirmed in contemporary terms. Paul is, at best, a mixed bag with regard to his views of social structures and human relationships.

In 1 Corinthians 14, Paul says, "Women should be silent in the churches." Some scholars are quick to point out that Paul was addressing himself to a specific situation with limited applicability. Others suggest that the passage in question may not even be Pauline in authorship but an interpolation added by an editor at another time. That is all well and good, but our problem is that those verses are still there. So we are stuck with what to make of this admonition, offensive as it is, and no amount of intellectual circumlocution or scholarly tap dancing can erase the hundreds of years of discrimination against women that have resulted from this passage's inclusion in the canon.

No amount of intellectual circumlocution or scholarly tap dancing can erase the hundreds of years of discrimination against women that have resulted from this passage's inclusion in the canon.

What are we to say to these instructions, and how can we understand them in our time? First, it needs to be understood that these letters were written to specific situations where a problem had arisen in a particular church setting. Every church has its peculiar characters, its somewhat heretical members who push the envelope and test the limits of the church's tolerance. Evidently someone in the Corinthian congregation had gotten out of hand and Paul felt impelled to establish some order in the midst of chaos, albeit with a heavy hand. The letter's injunction against free speech for women in the congregation is not meant to be for all time and for all places. It is specific to the Corinthian church.

But I do not think that we misunderstand Paul, nor that anything is lost in translation. I think we say too much if we say that Paul did not intend to quiet women in worship. If Paul were to have had his way, women in church would keep silent—period. Paul was a Jew of the first century, and to make of him a twentieth-century man sensitive to the needs and gifts of women within our contemporary understandings is to do a terrible disservice to Paul and to his advice to the Corinthian Christians.

> *Paul was a Jew of the first century, and to make of him a twentieth-century man sensitive to the needs and gifts of women within our contemporary understandings is to do a terrible disservice to Paul and to his advice to the Corinthian Christians.*

Let's call a spade a spade. Paul's view of women was shaped by the patriarchal culture and faith of his day. He believed that women should keep silent in church just as women kept silent in the synagogue. He was not a trailblazer for feminist issues. I would say Paul is not at his best when he writes to the Corinthians that women should keep silent in religious matters.

He was better when he said that in the Christian church there should be neither male nor female, slave nor free. He was better when he said that "just as woman came from man, so man comes through woman [and] all things come from God" (1 Cor. 11:12).

But in other respects his understandings regarding women are time and culture bound, reflecting more of Paul's biases, addressed to specific problems within the church at a given time, than they are timeless expressions of the dimensions of the gospel of Jesus Christ with all its freeing and liberating power. Held under the light of the gospel, Paul's words and his advice for women to keep silent are not broad enough, not hopeful enough, not expansive enough to stand the test of what it is that we would understand Jesus' will to be in the matter of the role of women in the church.

Jesus, in every way, broke the mold in his relationships, and especially in his appreciation of the unique and special character of each woman whom he encountered.

Jesus, in every way, broke the mold in his relationships, and especially in his appreciation of the unique and special character of each woman whom he encountered,

— whether it be in his meeting with the woman at the well, whom he astounded by speaking with her about everything she ever did;

— or in his compassionate meeting with the woman taken in adultery in which he exposed the hypocrisy of those men who would stone her for her sin;

— or in his empathy for the woman who threw herself at his feet at the Last Supper and who anointed him for burial, to the shock and disapproval of his disciples.

In all of these encounters, in all of his dealings with women, Jesus saw to the heart of each woman. Beyond the cultural limitations of his day and even some of the religious teachings of his native Judaism, Jesus consistently opted for what was hospitable, welcoming, and uplifting. That a woman was a woman was never an impediment to Jesus' way of treating her as a unique person of special worth, worthy of his time and full attention.

> *The dimensions of the gospel hold a higher hope for us than we have yet realized, a closer community of love and affection than we have yet attained.*

The kind of church I imagine Jesus being most proud of would be one in which all people are celebrated and employed in the tasks of Christian discipleship without concern for whether we are man or woman. Paul was undeniably right when he described the Christian church as a special community of love and acceptance, distinct from the secular world's values, a place of respite and peace where people are accepted simply for who they are, as a child of God, neither slave nor free, male nor female.

I believe the dimensions of the gospel hold a higher hope for us than we have yet realized, a closer community of love and affection than we have yet attained. We are called as Christians to be Christ-like in our dealings with one another, especially within the church, and to reflect the way of Jesus in our reception of one another. So we as God's people are called

— to employ women in the tasks of ministry;
— to ordain women as officers, priests, and ministers of the Word and Sacrament;
— to hear them as they speak;
— to hear them not with tolerance, but with apprecia-

tion for the gifts God has given them to speak with
authority and truth.

We need to do this not because it is in vogue. We need to
do it because in that ultimate commonwealth of God
toward which we are moving, that's the way things will be.
We may be Jew and Greek, male and female, but there will
be no regarding anyone as either Jew or Greek, slave or
free, male or female with any of the earthly discriminations
or roles that attend such designations, for we will all be one
in Christ Jesus. It might not have been time for Paul to
announce that vision in the first century, but by the Holy
Spirit it most certainly is time to claim it now.

Sometimes men stand in the way of women being rec-
ognized for who they are and for the gifts they bring to
life. And sometimes it is women who stand in the way of
each other. Discrimination is an equal opportunity demon.
But all of the standing-in-the-way in the world will not
prevent the eventual coming of a day of greater justice for
women in every aspect of life, not just in the church. That
is God's intention, that we all may be able to speak and be
heard in whatever venue God has given us gifts in which
to serve.

> *Sometimes men stand in the way of women being rec-*
> *ognized for who they are and for the gifts they bring*
> *to life. And sometimes it is women who stand in the*
> *way of each other. Discrimination is an equal oppor-*
> *tunity demon.*

In the meantime, in this imperfect world short of heaven,
we work on language in the church, and we call women to
the tasks of ministry and Christian service. We discover new
dimensions of God's relationship with us in feminist read-

ings of the Scriptures and theology. We try to model in our words and actions an appreciation for each other that considers not the source but the intention, not the gender but the wisdom, not the person but the soul that speaks and reflects the voice and heart of Jesus.

With no apologies to Paul—in fact, in firm contradiction of him—women must not be silent in church, in society, in politics, in the judiciary, in children's issues, in marital relations, in business and finance, in education and housing, in medicine, and in international relations until such time as the world reflects more of that commonwealth of God where we are headed.

So let both men and women speak in church and in every corner of life until that day comes, the day when justice is done and no one is judged in any respect except by whether or not they reflect in their life the love and justice of Jesus Christ.

Chapter Three

The Problem of Mistrust

One of the most familiar benedictions in both Judaism and Christianity is the Mizpah blessing. Its simple yet comforting words, "May the Lord watch between you and me when we are absent one from the other," seem to express the desire for a heavenly blessing of communion with God when friends are parted from one another. In reality the text is a non-aggression pact born of wariness and mistrust between two antagonists, Jacob and his father-in-law, Laban. In that context, the "watching" that God is invited to keep is more like sentry duty than heavenly protection or safekeeping. At stake is how peace can be made between bitter adversaries when there is no true peace between them.

One of the challenges of the text is that it is only a portion of an ongoing saga found in Genesis 27-35 in which Jacob is the central figure. In order for the listener to understand the meaning of the blessing, it must be set into its place in the larger story of which it is a part. This requires a retelling of the events leading up to the meeting at Galeed. Since the story is long, I have chosen to highlight it and to update it with anachronistic contemporary references. While many hearers of the sermon will not know the background, some will, which is why a lively retelling of it will put everyone, biblical student and new believer alike, on even ground.

The conflict with the text is its familiar interpretation in the church among those who do not know its biblical source and the true purpose it serves in its setting. The preacher's task is to find a way to proclaim the truth that this blessing proclaims, that old enemies can make peace, even imperfect peace, in an imperfect world.

Imperfect Peace

Genesis 31:44-55 IN THE LAST HALF OF THE BOOK OF Genesis, there is a soap opera. It is the story of Jacob, Rachel, Leah, and Laban, and it leaves today's TV soap operas in the dust. The plot is convoluted, as all such dramas are, and the characters are tossed and turned by their selfishness, greed, loves, and lusts.

In the story, Jacob is on the lam from Canaan, having deceived his father, Isaac, stolen the birthright of his brother Esau, and been threatened by a plot against his life. He makes his way to a little town called Haran, where when his eyes fall on a woman named Rachel it is love at first sight.

> *In the story, Jacob is on the lam from Canaan, having deceived his father, Isaac, stolen the birthright of his brother Esau, and been threatened by a plot against his life. He makes his way to a little town called Haran, where when his eyes fall on a woman named Rachel it is love at first sight.*

He strikes a deal with Rachel's father, Laban, and they agree that if Jacob's a good boy, works hard in the family business, and proves his worth as a son-in-law, he may have Rachel's hand in marriage—after seven years. But the father-in-law is a wily old fox, suspecting that he can put one over on Jacob the way Jacob has put one over on his old man. When the seven years have passed and the time has come for the wedding ceremony, Jacob is deceived, perhaps by too much wine and a heavy wedding veil that covers all the charms of his bride. After the vows are said, the ink is dry on the wedding license, and the copies are filed at the county clerk's office, Jacob realizes he has made a mistake.

He has been duped. His father-in-law substituted the older of his two daughters, Leah, in the place of her younger sister, Rachel. I grew up not too awfully far from the Ozarks, and sometimes you hear of this sort of thing down there, but it's not what you expect from the Bible!

When Jacob realizes what has happened he is hopping mad. So he goes to his father-in-law to demand restitution. Another deal is arranged: in exchange for a second seven years of work in the family business, Jacob may have both brides.

This might have been a tolerable arrangement for Jacob, but the sisters were not too excited about it. Not only are they upset with their father for the deception involved in their marriages, being treated like chattel as they were, but Leah is hurt that Jacob is not in love with her, and Rachel is jealous that Leah has first dibs on her man. Moreover, Leah gives birth to seven children before Rachel gives birth to her first. At every level there is dysfunction, sibling rivalry, paternal rejection, and tension in the marriage . . . uh, marriages.

At last, Jacob, Leah, Rachel, and their twelve children decide that they must make a break for it. They want out of the suffocating arrangement of living so close to family, and the deception and double-dealing to which they have been subjected. So they leave town late one night; the camels loaded, the trunks brimming full.

Now it might have been hard enough for Laban to lose his best and cheapest worker, Jacob, *and* his two daughters, *and* his twelve grandchildren, but what made things much more complicated was that Rachel, unbeknownst to Jacob, tried to feather her nest a little bit by stealing a few trinkets, some household statues, from her father's home just to spite Laban. And Laban is not about to let anyone steal from him.

At last the whole thing comes to a head at a little out-of-the-way place called Galeed, in what would be known as Mizpah in the hill country of Gilead. There at Galeed, at Mizpah, Laban brings his posse to find the things that have been stolen and to accuse Jacob of stealing them, and to do so without even so much as a "you have the right to remain silent."

Jacob denies stealing anything, not knowing what Rachel has done. "If I or any of mine have anything of yours," he swears, "that one shall be put to death. Go and search for yourself." So Laban searches Jacob's camp high and low.

Rachel, every bit her father's daughter, has outwitted Laban, for she has placed the stolen goods in a saddlebag on which she is sitting; when Laban comes into her tent, she claims that it is her time of the month and she cannot rise to greet him. Laban searches the tent, leaving the saddlebags to Rachel, and thereby bypasses the loot.

At last, Jacob—who has stolen his brother's birthright, who has lived by his wits on the lam all these years, who has unfinished business back home, who has family troubles aplenty (what with two bickering wives and twelve unruly children)—looks Laban, his father-in-law, straight in the eyes. Laban—who has pulled the rug out from under Jacob more than once, who has stolen twenty years of Jacob's life (seven years each for Leah and Rachel, and six years to get possession of some livestock), who has nary a straightforward word in his vocabulary—and Jacob the trickster stand before each other; they must make peace, lest they kill each other, eaten up by their mistrust.

They do something that is finally divinely inspired in this otherwise humanly uninspiring story. They gather some stones and make a mound of rocks—a marker, a memorial—as a place of remembrance.

What do they do? They do something that is finally divinely *inspired* in this otherwise humanly uninspiring story. They gather some stones and make a mound of rocks—a marker, a memorial—as a place of remembrance. They agree to disagree and yet to be bound together by the watchful eye of God. They will be separate, but they will remain one in covenant so that whatever God can do between them may yet be done. They bless the place of their meeting and of their parting.

"[May] the Lord watch between you and me, when we are absent one from the other," says Laban. It is barely a blessing, but it is a blessing. It is hardly peace, and yet it is peace.

> *It is barely a blessing, but it is a blessing. It is hardly peace, and yet it is peace.*

Nothing by these words is canceled or forgotten, and all that has transpired between them takes its awkward place in the journey they have traveled. But the blessing allows them to go on even with all that is unfinished between them. They settle on the reality that their argument cannot be settled and that only God can keep an uneasy peace between them.

That Mizpah blessing is probably the first blessing I ever learned in Sunday school. Isn't it one that almost all of us know by heart? "May the Lord watch between you and me, when we are absent one from the other."

But when you know the story this way, you realize that it is not all sweetness and light. It is a blessing borne of mistrust, bound by the need to make peace between two of God's children who have fundamental disagreements and good reason to want to keep an eye on each other. It settles only that the two of them will not hurt or scheme against each other any longer, and that all the rest shall be entrusted to God's watchful eye and care.

It is not well-resolved, this tension between them. And their predicament reminds us that sometimes on earth there is no way to settle a disagreement so fundamental between two people other than to call a truce and accept that the cost of continuing the battle is a price neither party is willing to pay.

The story is, of course, not only a soap opera, it is an archetype. Which is to say that we know this story. We may even have lived it or experienced it within our families, or have been part of it at work. It is not just a tale of long ago and far away, but a description of some of the relationships in which we find ourselves even today.

Sometimes in our relationships we have to settle for an uneasy peace that is barely peace at all but simply the best we can do, considering the cost of continuing the struggle. You know what I'm talking about.

> *Sometimes in our relationships we have to settle for an uneasy peace that is barely peace at all but simply the best we can do, considering the cost of continuing the struggle.*

There is some money in the family—not the Kennedy fortune, necessarily, but enough for two sisters to keep an eye on their interests through the years and dream of a better life when the inheritance becomes available. The one sister tells a lie or two along the way to the patriarch in the family, and when the inheritance is divided, the other sister has been left out because of the lies, the illusion having been created that she is not as needy as her sibling. Through the years thereafter there is brokenness between these two sisters. They do not speak of the money. In fact, they do not speak of many important things, for some things are better left unsaid. They live a kind of Mizpah peace, an uneasy truce between them, because for them it is better not to fight and by fighting lose the only close family they have than it is to have the satisfaction of settling the score.

It happens at work. Someone comes into your department as colleague and coworker who is nothing but trouble. She takes confidential information, spreads it throughout the office, and passes it on to clients. She tells you she has completed work assignments, but in truth she hasn't even started them. She butters up the boss, but behind his back she knifes him. She works the system in such a way that she gets credit for the work you've done. And when she is called on the carpet for the dishonesty and triangulation at which she's so adept, she tells higher-ups that jealous coworkers are trying to get her fired. As a coworker and not her boss, you're in a box. Short of stooping to her tactics, you find yourself cutting her a wide berth, making a Mizpah peace because you want to keep your job and because the price of getting even is just not the right way.

Maybe you have a teenager in the family who is long on rebellion and short on common courtesy. Psychologists call it "individuation," but in the family it usually feels more like global thermonuclear war.

Maybe you have a teenager in the family who is long on rebellion and short on common courtesy. Psychologists call it "individuation," but in the family it usually feels more like global thermonuclear war. He leaves his clothes piled high on the floor of the closet and expects you to do hide-and-seek to find them and get them into the washing machine. Money is missing from your pocketbook, and there's no other viable suspect. His friends are a mystery to you, because he doesn't tell you much of anything about with whom he is spending his time, and more and more time is spent away from home. Any inquiry into his whereabouts or the inconsistencies of what he tells you leads to a shouting match that hardly seems worth the effort anymore, there've been so many. You have come to a kind of Mizpah peace, hardly peace at all, except that it allows you some breathing space, some time not expended in battle. It is peace made in the hope that something better may come in time, even if the current stalemate is nearly intolerable; but having tried everything else, what is left except for the relationship to be abandoned altogether? That is a terrible price to pay.

This kind of peacemaking is interim at best. It is living as Jeremiah described it—as if there is peace when there is no peace. Will it hold? Maybe; maybe not. Is it a compromise? Most decidedly. But it is the best that can be done under the circumstances, and sometimes it is the only realistic option that is left. But maybe that's not always so bad.

In one church where I served, there was a member of my congregation who was an alcoholic, a recovering alcoholic, an AA alcoholic, a zealous and proselytizing AA alcoholic. I don't think I had been in that church for more than a week when he dropped by my office to introduce himself and tell me his drinking history. He offered to be a resource to anyone in the church who had a drinking problem. He took me to an open meeting the first chance he could, and he kept me abreast of all that was happening in his local "Twelve Step" program.

He had been sober for more than a dozen years when I first met him, and I learned from him that he had made a

Fritz taught me that he had drawn a line in the sand, piled some stones in the Mizpah of his heart, said a blessing, and agreed not to cross over that line anymore—respecting those opposing powers in his life.

certain peace with the alcohol that had threatened to consume his life. He made peace by doing what all "Twelve Step" alcoholics do: he acknowledged the power of alcohol in his life. And he acknowledged that, alone, he was powerless to overcome his drinking without help from a higher power. My parishioner taught me that he had drawn a line in the sand, piled some stones in the Mizpah of his heart, said a blessing, and agreed not to cross over that line anymore—respecting those opposing powers in his life. As long as he lived, he did not cross that line, did not dismantle a stone, nor renege on his blessing.

I would have wished for this man a healthier life, a life in which an occasional drink was not a problem, a life less haunted by shadows and temptations. But that was not meant to be. And the uneasiness of a Mizpah blessing was the best he could muster this side of heaven.

The story of the Mizpah blessing reminds us that some things don't get resolved in this life. Some disagreements go on for years, some for a lifetime. And some are never resolved; they just come to a stalemate. In the real world in which the Bible is steeped, human passions, human anger, and human frustration are acknowledged the way they sometimes are—chronic, ongoing, and unsettled.

There are in the Scriptures happily-ever-after stories, peace agreements that are kept, angers that are laid aside, hatreds that are resolved, and enemies who become friends. But not so in the thirty-first chapter of Genesis. There, two old enemies face each other and part fundamentally unchanged, except that they have agreed to pile some stones as a memorial to the promise that they will not fight anymore, and the rest they will leave to God. God, who will watch between them. God, who will be their witness. God, who will finally settle at another time and with wiser judgment what they cannot.

The story has no soaring inspiration to offer. No *deus ex*

machina to come down from the clouds and make things all right. No wonderful resolution of the distrust that has torn this family and these men apart. Just Jacob and Laban parting company and not looking back, so that they can get on with their lives.

But maybe that can be a kind of inspiration to us nonetheless, to know that while some things in this life can never be settled and concluded once and for all, they can be left to a higher wisdom to watch and protect, to settle and finish.

> *This side of heaven, maybe the best that we can say, the only blessing we can muster, the only closure we can find, is to leave it to God.*

"May the Lord watch between you and me, when we are absent one from the other." In the battles that we cannot win, in the struggles that we will not finish, in the relationships that we cannot fix (this side of heaven), that may be the best that we can say to another, the only blessing we can muster, the only closure we can find—to leave it to God. It is imperfect peace, but it is peace enough.

So, in all that is unsettled, may the Lord watch between you and me, when we are absent one from the other.

Chapter Four

Homosexuality

*Abortion and homosexuality are among the most controversial
issues of the church in the latter part of the twentieth century. At
the root of our passions about these issues lies our understanding of
the authority of Scripture. Unfortunately, recent years of debate
on both topics have left faithful people at an impasse, unable to
resolve their differing understandings of the Bible's guidance in
both matters.*

*I have chosen in this sermon to look not only at the authority
of Scripture, but also at the authority of the Holy Spirit as a
help in considering the issue of homosexuality. Most of the heat
and too little of the light on the matter has centered on what the
Scriptures say at a literal level about homosexuality, with too
little hermeneutical consideration of how those scriptures are to
be understood or applied today. Scholarly debate and biblical
study have added a great deal of helpful information in recent
years on interpreting the relatively small number of passages
that actually address homosexuality. Nevertheless, this scholarship is so often ignored, denied, or rejected within the church
that it seems clear that reason may not prevail in considering
the matter. Even reasonable and faithful people can be overcome
by passion, especially when their minds are decided from the
outset.*

*We know what the Holiness Code has to say about homosexual-
ity. We have heard Paul on the matter. We know that Jesus does
not address the issue at all. And we know what social scientists and
psychologists are saying about homosexuality, and even what gay
and lesbian people are telling us about themselves. Has anyone
heard from the Holy Spirit? In the sermon that follows, I try to
discern something of what that Spirit might be leading us to say
and to do.*

To Lie with a Male
As with a Woman

Leviticus 18:22;
Acts 8:26-40

WILLIAM SLOANE COFFIN HAS SUG-gested that within the modern church no issue since slavery has had the potential for divisiveness as has the issue of homosexuality.[1] Presbyterians, Episcopalians, Methodists, Roman Catholics, Lutherans—Christians from every part of the denominational spectrum have addressed themselves to the question of what is a Christian response to the reality of same-sex sexual expression in human life. One thing is for sure, no amount of religious approbation or disapproval has changed the fact that some people find themselves attracted to others of the same sex, both for sexual expression and for affectional commitment.

> One thing is for sure, no amount of religious approbation or disapproval has changed the fact that some people find themselves attracted to others of the same sex, both for sexual expression and for affectional commitment.

In general, the response of most Christian denominations has been that homosexuality is sin, based on the few passages of Scripture that refer to it.[2] One of the most clear and direct is the passage found in Leviticus 18:22: "You shall not lie with a male as with a woman, it is an abomination." To be fair, most reasoned theological discussions of homosexuality recognize that it is not the most heinous of sins and that its identification as sin should not lead to legal discrimination against homosexuals in the secular world. But while homosexuality is not a greater sin than any other, most religious denominations cite its practice as a distinctive moral category that disqualifies a person for ordination or leadership in the church.

Gay and lesbian members of our churches call this duplicitous interpretation of Scripture hypocrisy. They rightly point out that other sins of Leviticus identified as offensive to God and as an abomination (*toevah* in Hebrew), such as eating pork or misusing incense, do not disqualify a person from ordination. Why should homosexuality be set apart as the most offensive of all sins?

The issue of homosexuality just doesn't go away, even though many in the church feel that the peace, unity, and purity of the church may be destroyed by this single issue.

Not long ago, someone told me that he was tired of all the talk about sex in the church because he found himself "losing interest in it." I laughed and thought I should get him together with another person who told me, "I've taken up golf, and found it to be like sex with my wife. I'm not very good at it, but I keep trying anyway."

Thank goodness we can laugh about our humanity, part of which is our sexuality. We usually take sex too seriously. We've taken it so seriously that we've taken it out of its context in the Scriptures, enshrined it, built temples to it, laden it with importance and meaning that is greater than is there. We have written its prohibitions and abominations in gold leaf, and embellished it with decoration, as if God's primary concern above all else is how we express our attraction and love for another person with our bodies.

A closer look at the Scriptures suggests that we in the church tend to emphasize only those sexual prohibitions that cause us the most fear, the ones we find most threatening to our own sense of security. We have tucked away and forgotten those that seem insignificant to us. In the

Levitical passage, sexual relations are prohibited between a man and a woman even in marriage when a woman is menstruating. By what authority have we dismissed that prohibition but preserved and elevated the other? We conveniently disregard the abundant passages in Scripture that relate to possessions, to money, and their place in our lives, as we worship, adore, and find our security in them rather than in God. I have heard it said that one in every five sayings of Jesus in the Gospels deals with the inherent danger of possessions and their power to overtake our lives. Jesus, on the other hand, never even mentions homosexuality.

> *A closer look at the Scriptures suggests that we in the church tend to emphasize only those sexual prohibitions that cause us the most fear, the ones we find most threatening to our own sense of security. We have tucked away and forgotten those that seem insignificant to us.*

We cannot infer from that fact that Jesus had no concern for homosexuality, anymore than we can assume that since he does not mention rape, incest, or child abuse he had no concern for them, or would not today. We do know that Jesus blessed and honored marriage through his presence at the marriage at Cana, and in his teachings on the sanctity of marriage and the undesirability of divorce, but that gives us no better understanding of what he might have thought or said about homosexuality by inference. We simply do not know what Jesus thought of the matter.

I wish the comparatively few passages that deal with homosexuality in the Scriptures were not there. They are passages that have caused us tremendous dissension and pain in the church—those passages, and the ones that tolerate slavery,[3] forbid women a voice in the church (1 Cor.

14:34), condone violence and warfare in God's name (e.g., Psalm 137:9), and order marriage in favor of a man's superiority over his wife as opposed to a mutuality within their relationship (Col. 3:18). I wish all those passages were not there. They confuse our faith. They fly in the face of reason. They defy the way we understand the world and experience it from a twentieth-century, scientific, and rational point of view. Don't get me wrong; that is not a reason to reject them, simply because reason teaches us otherwise. In order to question any teaching of Scripture, we must be able to show that there is a higher claim in the gospel that supersedes it.

> *In order to question any teaching of Scripture, we must be able to show that there is a higher claim in the gospel that supersedes it.*

In that vein, we arrive at the heart of our disagreements within the church about the teachings of the Bible on homosexuality. The issue is how we interpret Scripture. Some will say that the Scriptures have a fixed and singular fundamental meaning. There is, in other words, a single and definite interpretation, a timeless and immutable truth, and our purpose is to discover it, write it in stone, and observe it. This is the point of view that says, "The Bible says it. I believe it. And that's that."

But I believe that the only fixed and singular immutable truth is God. The witness of the Scriptures is that God has chosen to be known in many and various ways. And the Holy Spirit continues to reveal new understandings of God in our daily experience. Ours is a God who, unlike any other worshiped on earth, has chosen to become flesh and has dwelt among us.

We read the Scriptures with the eyes of faith, and allow

its words to speak to our hearts. We also allow the tradition of centuries in the church, and our reason and intellect to inform our faith, believing that God uses all these things to make God's own self known.

> *The watershed event in the unfolding story of God's creative work among us was Jesus Christ, God's limitless expression of love and sacrifice given to us as a gift to draw all people to himself.*

There is a broad and sweeping movement in the Bible that describes a direction for the creation that God has set into motion. From Genesis 1 to Revelation 22, there is an authoritative witness to the shaping and forming of a God who creates the world, loves it, and who reconciles, sacrifices, and covenants with the earth and its people. That God moves us toward a unity and peace that we have not fully achieved. As the *Presbyterian Brief Statement of Faith* declares, "In sovereign love, God created the world good and makes everyone equally in God's image, male and female, of every race and people, to live as one community. But we rebel against God; we hide from our Creator. Ignoring God's commandments, we violate the image of God in others and ourselves, accept lies as truth, exploit neighbor and nature, and threaten death to the planet entrusted to our care."

The watershed event in the unfolding story of God's creative work among us was Jesus Christ, God's limitless expression of love and sacrifice given to us as a gift to draw all people to himself.

Our problem is that we get hung up on things that are not central to that gospel. There are so few references to homosexuality in all of the Scriptures that a reasonable person might wonder why the church has fixed on and divides itself over a matter that Jesus himself never addressed. I wonder if a century from now the church will look back on this period in our life together and wonder why we said and did such mean things to each other, why we cut from the body of Christ faithful people who sought to love and serve their Lord but who were prohibited on the basis of an arbitrary application of a very few scriptures that by sheer volume alone are not central to our faith, and that by any measure of Jesus' attention to them were of little weight in the great scheme of things in the commonwealth of God.

Many faithful people have loved and served their Lord, and found as well that they were homosexual. The church would be the poorer if our gay and lesbian members, our officers, priests, and ministers were not offering their gifts in service of the God who gave them life and breath and the vocation that is surely theirs.

Whose service might we have excluded? Wonderful composers (whose music we use in worship) such as Francis Poulenc, Leonard Bernstein, and Camille Saint-Saens: They were all homosexual. Should we ignore their music, deny their gifts, withhold their praise of God simply because they inherited a slightly different genetic code than the majority?

> *It is simply amazing what God can do in the lives of those who seem least likely to us but whom God seems ready to call long before we might.*

Or Michelangelo, should we hide his works? Or Cardinal Newman, should we ignore his accomplishments? They, too, were servants of God. Should we excise from our consciousness such marvelous people of faith, like Dag Hammerskjöld? Or those whose accomplishments have so enriched our lives, such as James Baldwin, Margaret Fuller, Willa Cather, Edith Hamilton, or even King James I for whom the famous version of the Bible is named?

It is simply amazing what God can do in the lives of those who seem least likely to us but whom God seems ready to call long before we might. When the Spirit of God moves in such surprising ways as this, we must take notice.

In the story of the baptism of the Ethiopian eunuch (Acts 8), the voice of the Holy Spirit speaks in a surprisingly new way about the one who is a sexual outcast, and his place in the assembly of God's people. The story goes like this: Philip, one of the apostles, was sent by the Holy Spirit to take the gospel to the Samaritans. On his way the Spirit ordered Philip to a certain road where an Ethiopian eunuch was traveling, the chancellor of the exchequer in Queen Candace's court.

> *About that time they were passing a small stream—a good place for a baptism—and the eunuch asked Philip, "What is to prevent me from being baptized?"*

The Torah, the same law that proclaims homosexuals to be an abomination to God, forbade eunuchs from entering the assembly of the Lord (Deut. 23:1). In our frame of reference they couldn't become members of the synagogue or the church; they were not acceptable by virtue of their sexual difference from the majority.

Philip, however, was sent to this Ethiopian eunuch, who was riding along in his chariot, reading the prophet Isaiah. Philip explained the passage from Isaiah and proclaimed the gospel, the good news of Jesus Christ, to him and it moved this eunuch to the core.

About that time they were passing a small stream—a good place for a baptism—and the eunuch asked Philip,

"What is to prevent me from being baptized?" It's an interesting way of phrasing the question, and of asking to be baptized, don't you think? And it makes me wonder, is there anything that stands in the way of any of us being baptized?

Specifically, in the case of the eunuch, the legal answer to his question is found in Deuteronomy 23:1: "No eunuch is to be admitted to the assembly of the Lord." There was clear direction with regard to what to do in the matter of the eunuch and his being unfit to enter the assembly of God's people. Was there anything to prevent him from being baptized? Yes, the very fact that he was a eunuch, a condition over which he did not have control and which he could not alter!

But Philip was not a legalist. So, prompted by the Spirit, which is the primary actor in this story, Philip baptized the eunuch, and the eunuch went on his way rejoicing.

The Holy Spirit then "beamed" Philip over to Azotus to pick up his evangelistic mission where he left off, which is the peculiar way Luke has in Acts of telling us that what was happening was not the work of human faith and intellect, nor of insubordinate disregard for the law, but an inspired action of God's power and wisdom.

In this story, we see a sexual outcast, rejected by a specific Deuteronomic passage and who was not permitted entrance to the assembly of God's people, allowed entrance and welcomed into the baptized community of faith as a follower of Jesus Christ.

I think the gospel's spacious hope is that all God's people in all of the diversity in which we come—white and black and yellow and red; men, women, and children; people from North and South and East and West; eunuchs, gays, straights, and celibates—will all sit at the table in the commonwealth of God, that place where there is, as Paul says, neither Jew nor Greek, neither slave nor free, neither male nor female; for we are all one in Christ Jesus (Gal. 3:28).

I think the gospel is drawing us toward unity and peace

even in a time when there is no unity or peace to be found in the church. And I say that not on the basis of what I see, but on the basis of what I do not yet see, of what I believe is the gospel's witness that in God's time there shall be such a time. I believe that—not in my lifetime perhaps, but in God's time—the church will welcome and ordain homosexual persons, men and women who sincerely believe themselves to be called to ministry as priests and ministers of the Word and Sacrament.

Will they live up to it? Can they lead an exemplary life? How well do any of us do that? We do it as best we can.

> I think the gospel is drawing us toward unity and peace even in a time when there is no unity or peace to be found in the church. And I say that not on the basis of what I see, but on the basis of what I do not yet see, of what I believe is the gospel's witness that in God's time there shall be such a time.

A pastor friend of mine tells the story of visiting a gay man, a member of his congregation, who was in the hospital and desperately ill with AIDS. The man was literally gasping and laboring for every breath. His lungs were full of fluid, his body wracked with fever. There were not many words he could say without a tremendous effort on his part, nor could he be heard without close listening on the part of his pastor. Toward the end of their visit, this man, struggling for every word, whispered to my friend, "At my funeral be sure to have everyone sing 'I'll Praise My Maker While I've Breath.'"

Not everyone will agree with me, I know. But I look to the day when the church not only finds no reason why one whose faith like that may not be baptized, but also one whose faith like that may not also be counted worthy to be ordained in the service of God. Until that day, we wait to discover more light to shine in our darkness, more faith to illumine our lives, and more responsiveness to the Holy Spirit to welcome the outcast and stranger into our midst.

Hasten that day, O Lord, when blest is the tie that binds our hearts in Christian love.

Chapter Five

Vengeance and Forgiveness

One of the more obscure but, nevertheless, more perplexing biblical stories is that of the revenge of Dinah's honor. As is often the case in unfamiliar biblical stories, a lively retelling of the story in the sermon may be the best way to introduce the congregation to the problem inherent in the text. I have chosen to retell it seasoned with the salt of contemporary and anachronistic references to make it more vivid for the listener.

The text bears an ethical embarrassment. Jacob's sons take revenge on the city of Shechem by slaughtering disabled men ostensibly to avenge the honor of their sister. In reality, it is the sons' honor that is avenged and their entire family's long-term security that is sacrificed. The story is so offensive that its very presence in the canon is surprising.

One aspect of the text that must receive some attention is the way in which Dinah is herself treated as chattel. She has no voice in the story, even though the story revolves around the violation of her personhood. As a way of dealing with this silence and the injustice involved in her lack of voice, in this sermon I have chosen to let Dinah speak. What would she have said to this matter?

The offensiveness of the text speaks for itself, culminating in Jacob's eloquent statement of the dilemma his sons' behavior has created for all of his family. This is a fact that cannot be avoided. The question of whether revenge is ever an acceptable recourse for people of faith is central to the ethical dilemma the story presents. In that sense the text offers an important teaching event, as the preacher wrestles with what in the passage is instructive for faith.

It is always awkward to juxtapose the Old and New Testaments, skipping centuries and crossing contexts. But in this case the issue of revenge cuts across all time barriers, and Jesus' words can, in fact, address precisely the issue raised by the Genesis text. Placed against the model of Jesus' own words of forgiveness from the cross, and his teaching of forgiveness of enemies (even those who would spitefully use us or steal from us), the issue of revenge is placed into a new light. Those who would be disciples of Jesus must deny the instinct to take revenge; they must take up the difficult cross of faithfulness, and follow the example of forgiveness Jesus lived as well as taught.

The Revenge of Dinah's Honor

Genesis 34; Matthew 5:38-48

THERE IS NOT MUCH that is edifying in the story of the revenge of Dinah's honor. It is embarrassing on many counts, one of which is that it is awkward for polite people and Sunday preaching, in that the story includes a rape, reference to circumcision, the massacre of all the men of a city, the plundering of all their worldly treasures as well as women and children, and the exposure of a morally weak Jacob. It's also a story that ends with no resolution, only a question that leaves us hanging about what redeeming social value we are to gain from it.

In a nutshell, this is the story: Jacob and his family have moved to the land around the town of Shechem. They will be farmers there. Dinah, who is Jacob's daughter, goes out to visit some girlfriends one day, and while she is on her way she is raped by young Shechem, for whom the town is named.

After the rape, Shechem tells his father, Hamor, that he would like to marry Dinah; whether this is because Shechem is riddled with guilt or because he has fallen in love, or just because he wants to have Dinah at his disposal, we do not know. Nonetheless, Hamor and Shechem go to Jacob to discuss a dowry and to see what terms can be arranged for the marriage. But the terms are actually dictated by Jacob's sons, who, knowing of the rape, have hatched a plot to avenge their sister's honor.

As a condition of the bride price, all the men of the town of Shechem agree to the Jewish ritual of circumcision and thereby overcome the stigma of being pagans. But we know this is a hollow requirement, because three days after the mass circumcisions, Jacob's sons come to the city by stealth and slaughter the men, who are unable to defend themselves, still smarting as they are from their surgery. Then, Jacob's clan take from the city all the booty they can load into their station wagons and U-Hauls, including all the women and children.

As the story ends, Jacob complains to his sons that they have made his life difficult by this Pearl Harbor attack, and how will he be able to live with his neighbors, who will surely distrust every Jew from now on. To which the sons answer in uncharacteristically frank terms for the Bible: "[But what about our sister?] Should our sister be treated like a whore?" (Gen. 34:31).

> *What is so worthwhile about this story that it has survived all the editing and preserving and painstaking copying over the centuries that has gone into delivering the Bible into our hands? What, if any, redeeming social value is there to the revenge of Dinah's honor?*

It's perfectly obvious why this account might make anyone's list of least loved biblical stories. My guess is that few people even know it is in the Bible. As I was growing up, I never heard a preacher preach on this text, and no Bible study in which I have participated has ever looked too closely at this passage. I came upon it somewhat by chance as I was re-reading Genesis, and even though I have read it before, the implications of its gruesome assertions never seemed to hit home before. But now I am wondering what is edifying about it. What is so worthwhile about this story that over the centuries it has survived all the editing and preserving and painstaking copying that has gone into delivering the Bible into our hands? What, if any, redeeming social value is there to the revenge of Dinah's honor?

Scholars have not done much with this story. It is hardly a gold mine for theological inquiry. Most are as embarrassed and confused by the story's obscure point as are any of us. Some have suggested that this is really a story of tribal history, since it appears that the people of Shechem have been personified in the person of Shechem. The story might be a tribal explanation of poor relations with the people of Shechem. But even if it is tribal history, it is still not edifying, and something of history must lie at its roots.

Jacob comes off as a weak father, not very protective of his daughter, unable to control his sons, and passive in his complaints about the problems his sons have created by their aggression. The sons have taken a treasured sign of God's covenant in circumcision and used it deviously as a means to ensnare and disable Israel's enemy, a cynical act to say the least. And for modern hearers, the story seems peculiarly silent about the feelings of Dinah and her mother, Leah, with regard to what happens to Shechem and his father. Perhaps most offensive is the disproportionate level of revenge that Jacob's sons inflict on Shechem's men. It sounds like gang warfare in modern Los Angeles or Chicago. The stuff of which a *West Side Story* is written.

> *Move the characters around, change the place, and you have an archetypal story of violence that is played out again and again.*

Move the characters around, change the place, and you have an archetypal story of violence that is played out again and again. An urban gang takes revenge against another gang because of a drive-by shooting in which one of its members is injured. An otherwise pleasant afternoon at the ballpark becomes a melee when a batter heads for the pitcher's mound to take out his frustrations on the pitcher's face after a fastball dusts him from the plate. And so the benches empty. Israel launches an attack across the Lebanese border when it suspects a Hezbollah hideout. Your ten-year-old is angry because your seven-year-old keeps using his baseball mitt without asking permission; so one day the older kid just comes along and takes a hammer to the seven-year-old's Nintendo controls.

We see it in every level of social interaction, from our own families upward, the desire to get even, or even to get one-up on the opposition. It is evidently innate in the human character. We cannot stand to have our honor or our possessions compromised.

> *Of all the voices of violence involved in this dreary account, none that speak have much worthwhile to say. It is actually the silent voice that would, no doubt, be most eloquent. Dinah's voice.*

This is why the story of the rape of Dinah is such a dismal failure if its purpose is to show us a better way. It does not, except perhaps as a negative example of the futility of revenge, for the outcome does not advance anything in the human spirit. The result is summarized by Jacob when he says to his sons, "You have brought trouble on me by making me odious to the inhabitants of the land . . . ; my numbers are few, and if they gather themselves against me and attack me, I shall be destroyed . . ." (Gen. 34:30). Revenge, in other words, never ends a matter; it only complicates it. It only postpones settlement.

Of all the voices of violence involved in this dreary account, none that speak have much worthwhile to say. It is actually the silent voice that would, no doubt, be most eloquent. Dinah's voice. She of all the figures who count in this story would likely have the redeeming word, were she allowed to speak. And what might she say? What might her voice sound like? Perhaps something like this:

It was a disgrace, yes, what happened to me. But what happened after made it even worse. None of these men know what it is like, especially not my brothers. The disgrace was awful, but I was innocent. I knew that in my heart, although some tried to say I did something to bring it on, to tempt Shechem. I did nothing of the sort.

They were not thinking of me. They thought only of themselves. It was not my honor they avenged, but their own disgrace that they wanted to wipe out.

I trembled at the thought that my father and brothers would arrange for a marriage with the man who had so abused me. I pleaded with them against it. But I also knew that no man of Israel would have me, customs being such as they were. My only hope for honor as a woman was to be with Shechem. That may sound strange to you, but no woman of my time was valued on her own. Only in relation to a man could a woman have honor. And since no man of Israel would disgrace himself by marrying a disgraced woman, my choices were reduced to Shechem. I hated him for what he did, but at the same time he was my only chance to overcome what had happened.

My brothers were hotheaded. They were not thinking of me. They thought only of themselves. It was not my honor they avenged, but their own disgrace that they wanted to wipe out. They thought they were my protectors. They hated having the family name whispered in knowing tones around our village. And so they tricked the men of Shechem, disgracing the covenant God had made with us, by circumcising these pagans and then slaughtering them when they were vulnerable and unable to defend themselves. Where was the honor in that?

And where did it leave me? They took my husband—my only chance to live with honor—and killed him, leaving me a widow and living in disgrace again. The women and children of Shechem were left without their husbands and fathers, and now they will have nothing to do with me for the hatred they lay upon my head.

I cannot, I will not, understand these ways. For now my father is a pariah in the land. The rumors among the Perizzites and Canaanites are that our people are shifty and not to be trusted. And we lie vulnerable to the threat of our neighbors, who are on guard against us. My brothers are satisfied, they say. My father is worried. My mother just shakes her head. And I, I am alone, alone and sorrowful, for nothing I did deserved all this. And nothing, nothing, has really been settled at all.

Dinah's voice would possibly be the only voice of reason, the only voice in control. Hers would be the voice of suffering, and in spite of the suffering the only voice of hope. In her words can be heard echoes of Jesus' words when he said, "Love your enemies and pray for those who persecute you" (Matt. 5:44).

> *Revenge is never an ennobling enterprise. There is not much of the human spirit that is furthered by what we do in the heat of passion or the rage of anger.*

As we might expect, the words of Dinah and the words of Jesus are drowned out by the cries for revenge in each of us. It is somehow always gratifying to see those who have wronged us fall. We know that. But in the quiet after the revenge is over, like that conversation between Jacob and his sons, we know that our retaliation is not the end of the matter. Revenge is never an ennobling enterprise. There is not much of the human spirit that is furthered by what we do in the heat of passion or the rage of anger. Our revenge only opens the door to our enemy's retaliation.

There are times when it is important to stand up for our rights. Times when we are injured and justice must be sought. Times when others take advantage of us and it is necessary to seek redress. Women especially have too often been told not to assert themselves in situations where they have been wronged. So we should not misconstrue Jesus' words—to love our enemies and pray for those who persecute us—as a mandate to live life as a doormat. There are times and occasions when the just thing to do is to fight against the wrong being perpetrated against you.

It is an imperfect world, and rarely do we find perfect solutions to the problems created by human passions. They just run too deep. If a member of my family were raped, violated, or abused, I know the power of the anger that would quickly rise within me, the murderous instinct that could be there. When someone with whom I work is falsely accused, maligned by another person, or hurt by something over which they had no control, I want to fight back with fair means or foul. And sometimes when I hear about the outrageously petty but mean things that people do to each other in the midst of a divorce—such as removing furniture from the house when the spouse is away at work, or using the kids as tools for spoiling a relationship with the ex—it makes me furious. It would make me want to retaliate and up the ante.

But then come those words of Jesus that are more sensible than I have sense, that are more reasoned than my reasoning, more passionately hopeful in the long run than my passionate retaliation: "Love your enemies and pray for those who persecute you, so that you may be children of your Father in heaven." He who hung from a cross and prayed, "Forgive them; for they know not what they do" (Luke 23:34 KJV), knew the price paid by the soul for revenge. It was he who taught that we should turn the other cheek, give away the coat as well as the cloak to the one who would take them from us. He taught this not because he was a pushover, or weak, or lacked spine or backbone, but because he knew that evil that is not returned will finally play itself out. He also knew that vengeance is not a human enterprise, but a cry to be raised to heaven. And there where peace is true shalom, where all is known and understood, where justice fairer than any we can mete is rendered, our cries are heard. "Vengeance," when all is said and done, "is mine, I will repay, says the Lord" (Rom. 12:19).

Jesus' words catch me short because in the end I know that my revenge is only temporary, only good until the next returned salvo. My anger is only for myself, and not a blow for justice. I can never end violence with hatred. That only comes with love, love wise enough, good enough, and patient enough to control revenge. For revenge never serves God; it only serves ourselves. It does not usher in justice; it only tips the balance of power for a time.

How do we overcome this impasse? Not easily. Perhaps not at all this side of heaven. I despair sometimes for the sake of us that we are so given to revenge. It seems so basic to our nature.

You want me to resolve this dilemma? Okay, I will: Love your enemies and pray for those who persecute you, so that you may be children of our God who is in heaven. Satisfied? Probably not, but it is a better answer than "Go and do likewise," go get your pound of flesh, go beat your enemy into submission, go up the ante and let your passions rule. The latter will satisfy for the moment, but the first answer has at least the chance of breaking the cycle.

At the end of the story of the revenge of Dinah, Jacob

complains to his sons that their retaliation has not settled the matter but has only tipped the scales of power for a while. The Canaanites and the Perizzites may well want to retaliate because of the threat that Jacob's people pose to their safety. And Jacob's sons look their father in the eye and ask, "But what of our sister; what of Dinah's honor? What of our family's name? Would you have left it that she would be treated like a whore?"

> *When all is said and done we are often left with bitter choices and imperfect decisions to make with regard to our anger, and in dealing with our passions.*

It is as good and as unsettling a place to leave it as we can have from this story, because when all is said and done we are often left with bitter choices and imperfect decisions to make with regard to our anger, and in dealing with our passions. Each of us must find the best way we can to settle with justice and with fairness the hurts we suffer at the hands of others, and to do so sometimes in the midst of circumstances that are neither just nor fair. The measure by which we judge ourselves and by which we are judged is the measure Jesus himself established, he who from the cross prayed for his enemies. "Love your enemies," he said, "and pray for those who persecute you, so that you may be children of our God who is in heaven."

Love our enemies? Love our *enemies*? God help us love our enemies!

Chapter Six

Universalism

*One of the issues with which every Christian wrestles is the theo-
logical issue of universalism. This is the question, Will everyone be
saved, or is the commonwealth of God a restrictive realm in which
"the gate is narrow, and the way is hard, that leads to life, and
those who find it are few"? Many fundamentalist and evangelical
Christians are motivated in their efforts toward evangelism by
both the Great Commission to "go . . . and make disciples of all
nations, baptizing them in the name of the Father and of the Son
and of the Holy Spirit," and also by the belief that those who do
not hear and accept the gospel will be lost to eternal damnation.
Other Christians believe that salvation is God's province alone
and that only God can sort out who is welcome in that divine commonwealth and who is not.*

*In June of 1996, the Southern Baptist Convention announced
its intention to establish a conversion mission to the Jews, a controversial decision that sets Southern Baptists apart from other
American Protestants, and Roman Catholics. Most others instead
have chosen to engage in ecumenical conversations with Jewish
leaders but not to seek to convert them. Since this is a theological
issue of no small significance, it is one that is worth considering
with a congregation.*

*Many Christians don't know what to think about other world
religions and popular secular ideologies. Some believe in a form of
Christian superiority that compares all other faiths unfavorably.
Others think that we all believe in the same God and that "we're
all trying to get to heaven anyway, so it really doesn't matter what
we believe."*

*The text, John 14:1-7, brings this issue into focus because of its
apparent clarity, yet contextually bound meaning. I have sought in
this sermon to maintain the tension between the claim the text*

makes in its naive meaning, "No one comes to the Father, except through me," while at the same time recognizing that all human seeking after God is seeking after an unfathomable mystery in which all language fails and all faith is proclaimed in the midst of wonder.

No One Comes to the Father Except Through Me

A<small>LMOST EVERY</small> C<small>HRISTIAN IS FAMILIAR</small>
with those glorious words of the four-teenth chapter of John's Gospel used so often in funeral services:

John 14:1-7

> Do not let your hearts be troubled. Believe in God, believe also in me. In my Father's house there are many dwelling places. If it were not so, would I have told you that I go to prepare a place for you? . . . I will come again and will take you to myself, so that where I am, there you may be also. (John 14:1-3)

They are comforting words, some of the highest and loftiest thoughts of our faith. Many of us have drawn solace from them as we have let go of people we love, in the hope of seeing them again in a better place and time, envisioning them in the dwelling places of heaven.

But at the end of that beautiful passage, which has given us a glimpse of the glory of everlasting life, there is a shift in mood that doesn't seem to fit. Thomas says to Jesus, "Lord we do not know where you are going. How can we know the way?"

"I am the way," answers Jesus, "and the truth, and the life. No one comes to the Father except through me." Now this last part is one of many passages in the Bible that I find I have a hard time accepting and understanding. It's one of the passages I have found most troubling. In fact, at times I have occasionally gone so far as to not read it in a funeral service where there were many people of other faiths present. It sounds insulting and arrogant on Jesus' part, exclusive and beneath him. "No one comes to the Father except through me."

On the other hand, I have to admit I am elitist enough to hear in that announcement the priority of Christianity over all other religions, and that has a kind of snobby cachet and parochial affirmation that appeals to my baser instincts. Nevertheless, I always come back to an embarrassment about this one phrase in an otherwise glorious promise of Jesus, and wonder what it is doing there spoiling everything.

What do we say in the face of all other faiths? Is Christianity the only way to God? Does no one come to God except through Jesus? "I am the way," he said, "and the truth, and the life. No one comes to the Father except through me."

> **What do we say in the face of all other faiths? Is Christianity the only way to God?**

It seems to me that all human beings in some way or another want to make sense of life and of life's experiences. When I go to the hospital to visit with people who are seriously ill, the two most common questions I am asked are, "What did I do to deserve this?" and "Why is this happening?" We don't like to think that the events of our life are random, inexplicable, or occur unjustly, so we look for links to our experience, something to make sense of it all.

The Greeks and Romans long ago saw life as strangely affected by the wars and passions of gods and goddesses who had all the frailties of the human condition. Rain, fertility, war, peace, and love were all governed by deities to whom these qualities were assigned. The Hebrew people believed in one true God and knew God to be Yahweh, who created all things and who ordered human life, a higher authority who took a special interest in the social, political, and historic events of a chosen race. Buddhism looks to a twelvefold path of enlightenment that negates the world and leads to a higher level of existence. Hindus worship many gods, including Vishnu, Shiva, and Brahma. Islam recognizes Abraham and Jesus as prophets, but places priority upon the teachings of Mohammed, the last and greatest of all the prophets. And Native American spirituality understands a Great Spirit to be behind all things, uniting humanity with star and moon, earth and sky. And thus, people of differing cultures and places in their own way and in their own time have attempted to understand what makes the world tick. As a friend once said to me, we all have three basic questions we want to answer in this life: Who am I? Where am I going? And who are all these other people?

Even science becomes a kind of religion in attempting to explain the mysteries of life. Dennis Overbye, in an editorial in *Time* magazine, points out this fact.

> The currency of science is not truth, but doubt, and paradoxically faith. Science is nothing if not a spiritual undertaking. The idea that nature forms some sort of coherent whole, a universe, ruled by laws accessible to us, is a faith. The creation and end of the universe are theological notions, not astronomical ones.[1]

When Jesus says "I am the way, and the truth, and the life. No one comes to the Father except through me," is he putting down all other ways of believing? Is he dismissing the possibility that we may come to God in any other way except through belief in Jesus Christ? Maybe and maybe not.

Jesus, and later the apostles, had to struggle against the pagan gods of Rome and the worship of idols, which was current in the world in which they lived. Many thought Christianity to be a form of Judaism. In fact, it wasn't until the gospel went to Antioch late in the first century that the followers of Jesus were known as Christians. Until that time they were simply known as followers of the Way. So, Jesus announced that he was the way, the truth, and the life. Threatening times call for extreme declarations.

> *There are times and seasons when it is important to declare where you stand over against the competing claims of would-be religions that also offer definitive explanations of the mysteries and order of life.*

How else do you differentiate a religion, except to lay claim for its distinctiveness? So perhaps Jesus was simply trying to make the point that sometimes you have to decide something once and for all. In this case, compared with the religions and mythologies of his time, Jesus was asserting the distinctiveness and priority of being his disciple, pre-empting even Judaism.

There are times and seasons when it is important to declare where you stand over against the competing claims of would-be religions that also offer definitive explanations of the mysteries and order of life.

There are still many pretenders to the throne of God that offer explanations behind the mystery of life. New Age consciousness, so popular in the West, waters down truth while glorifying mysticism at the expense of intellect. Crystal energy is touted as having healing power, so people buy trinkets and hang them around their necks to influence their lives. The Baha'i faith tries to put all religions together, like a spiritual mulligan stew, saying there is a little bit of divine truth in every faith, that all are imperfect expressions of a divine reality greater than we can understand. And don't many people think, "Well, we all believe in the same God anyway, so it doesn't really matter what you believe because we all want to get to the same place (meaning heaven)"? The problem is that this would come as startling news to a Hindu or a Jew, a Buddhist or a Muslim. We don't all believe in the same God as God is described in our differing scriptures. We understand the divine in different ways, and it does a discredit to the sincere beliefs of other faiths when we dismiss those differences so easily.

> *We understand the divine in different ways, and it does a discredit to the sincere beliefs of other faiths when we dismiss those differences so easily.*

Somehow, rather than dismiss the distinctiveness of other faiths, we need to find a way to honor those differences while preserving the claims of our own. That, it seems to me, is the spirit and thrust of the gospel, not intolerance and religious fanaticism, but humility, patience, and the strong power of love that knows God can make sense of all we have confounded, and that as sure as Jesus is the way, the truth, and the life, he is able to manifest that way and truth and life in many and various forms.

Our faith is that Jesus Christ was the Son of God and Savior of the world. He performed a unique and unrepeatable act of love and sacrifice on the cross, revealing the true nature of God's love. God raised him in power, and by his resurrection we know how great is God's ability to overcome evil and sin in this world. To know the story of Jesus is to have a special and beautiful knowledge of God and the way the universe hangs together, the meaning of the human experience, and the mystery that surrounds us all our days.

Our imperative is to share that story with all who do not know it, and with all who will hear it. It is still the way of salvation, to wholeness, and to communion with God, which is what salvation means, being whole and at one with

God. The Great Commission to go into all. the world baptizing in the name of the Father and of the Son and of the Holy Spirit is still our mandate.

But to interpret Jesus' saying, "No one comes to the Father except through me," as a polemic against all other religions is, I think, to say more than we know. In the case of every passage of Scripture, we have to weigh what is said with the measure of the whole force, spirit, and power of the gospel. The gospel never seems to me to identify as its greatest enemy other religions as we know them.

There are instead two enemies of the gospel that war against it. One is idolatry, the great sin of the Hebrew Scriptures; that is, worshiping human-made deities, like loving money, and work, and ambition, and status, and alcohol, anything that would become so important in a person's life that he or she would make any sacrifice for it, substituting what is earthly for what is heavenly. And the other enemy of the gospel is Satan and his legions, which is to say, evil and its power among us.

So far as I know, Jesus himself did not know other world religions as we know them. He must have been aware of Zoroastrianism, Roman mythology, and other pagan religions. But Jesus never speaks specifically of these religions in the Gospels. To place the burden of rejection of all other faiths for all time on this one saying, appearing only in John's Gospel, in the fourteenth chapter, is to ask it to bear too much weight.

So how ought we to think of other religions? We ought to think of them with respect and take them seriously. Who is to say that God, in God's infinite wisdom, does not work

So how ought we to think of other religions? We ought to think of them with respect and take them seriously.

through the cultures and beliefs of other people whose view of life is very different from ours? Are all the same? Of course not! "You will know them by their fruits," Jesus advised his disciples (Matt. 7:20). And elswhere John, in one of his letters, suggested that we "test the spirits to see if they are of God; for many false prophets have gone out into the world" (1 John 4:1). The idea is that simply because a religion has many adherents does not make it ultimate truth. The truth is in the quality of life that religion brings forth from its believers and whether, from a Christian point of view, that belief bears the marks and signs of the commonwealth of God, where the whole creation exists in praise of its Creator, and the people of every nation and culture do justly, love mercy, and walk humbly with their God.

Surely there is more than one way to name the name of Jesus Christ. And surely there must be more than one way to worship and honor him. Isn't he served and praised, for instance, wherever acts of justice and mercy and peacemaking are done? Aren't these the deeds that help to reveal him in our world?

> *The measure of worthiness to enter the precincts of heaven will not be whether each soul has made the proper confessional statement articulated in precisely the words prescribed by tradition, but whether we have fed the hungry, clothed the naked, visited the sick and imprisoned, and welcomed the stranger.*

Don't you remember how he described that vision of the end of time when all the nations will be gathered and judged? The measure of worthiness to enter the precincts of heaven will not be whether each soul has made the proper confessional statement articulated in precisely the words prescribed by tradition, but whether we have fed the hungry, clothed the naked, visited the sick and imprisoned, and welcomed the stranger. As we care for these, we care for him. Those who have served him in this way are surprised to discover that it is him for whom they have cared. To serve and honor him can be done without our even knowing.

Once, Jesus was told by his disciples that a man was casting out demons in his name and that the disciples forbade the man to do so because he was not following them. Jesus rebuked them, saying, "Do not stop him; for no one who does a deed of power in my name will be able soon afterward to speak evil of me. Whoever is not against us is for us" (Mark 9:38-40).

There was a permissiveness in Jesus that surprised his disciples and amazed his enemies. His way was one of drawing a circle so broad and so inclusive that even those who wished to stand outside it found themselves enveloped in it unexpectedly. What lines of exclusion Jesus drew were usually reserved for Pharisees and members of the temple elite, who themselves specialized in drawing lines to exclude others.

> *Might not even the rhythm of life, death, and resurrection writ throughout the creation and seen in the rising and falling of the seasons be a silent witness to his name without ever naming him as such?*

I wonder, if that is the case, whether it may not also be possible that he is present in the meditation and worship, the mantras and prayers of many people who do not know his name. Might not even the rhythm of life, death, and resurrection writ throughout the creation and seen in the rising and falling of the seasons be a silent witness to his name without ever naming him as such?

Jesus was not a stickler for creeds and formulations in quite the same way we are. He announced the approaching reign of God not by devising a formal declaration, but by announcing in a few brief words the need to repent and believe, the kingdom of God is at hand (Mark 1:15). Simple, basic, uncomplicated.

Is this too mystical, too heady, too generous—this understanding of the way to God that leads through Jesus Christ? Well, let me simplify it as best I can.

Joseph Campbell, who has done so much to make us familiar with mythology and the human search for meaning common to all cultures, was once asked by Bill Moyers why, after seeing so many commonalities in religions, one might believe there was more truth in one than another; why believe in the Christian assertion that God took flesh and dwelt among us in Jesus Christ? His answer was that this is the story we know, that other explanations do not usually move us in quite the same way because of our lack of symbols and meanings in our culture. "Why be a Christian?" he was asked. "Because you dance with the girl with whom you came," he said.

And while his answer is only a fraction of the reason why we would pursue our faith in Jesus Christ, a whimsical expression at best, it is a start. It is the story we know, and there is so much truth in it, so much of the way, so much of life, that in him our experience has shown us that his words are undeniably true—"I am the way, and the truth, and the life." If nothing in my experience or yours had ever shown that it was so, we could abandon it. But that is not the case, is it?

God has no doubt created an infinite number of ways to be known. And we reach and grasp and extend our arms heavenward to grab hold of the mysteries of life. But the unique claim of Christianity is that while other religions reach up to God, the God made known in Jesus Christ reaches down to

The unique claim of Christianity is that while other religions reach up to God, the God made known in Jesus Christ reaches down to us and is known in terms we can all understand.

us and is known in terms we can all understand. For God comes and dwells among us, full of grace and truth.

A lot of evil things have been done because of the idea that some Christians have had that when Jesus said, "No one comes to the Father except through me," it was some kind of license to bully and browbeat and force submission from everyone else in the world who thinks differently. The Crusades, the historical and ongoing persecution of Jews, the worst of Victorian mission efforts that were often really cultural expeditions (taking woolen underwear to the Hawaiian islanders, for instance)—these were all sincere but misguided, and often painful, misapplications of Jesus' saying.

"No one comes to the Father except through me," Jesus said. I think I will always rest uneasy with this saying. But maybe Gerard Sloyan's suggestion of how we understand this is the most helpful of all:

> Jesus must be proclaimed as the one way to God to whomever is willing to listen, while leaving the faith and the fate of those who have never heard the gospel to a God who is equal to the problem. The church will always be missionary because it is convinced it possesses in the gospel a peculiar treasure. . . . But [at the same time] there is a much greater trust in the providence of God nowadays and of God's mysterious ways of self-disclosure to all the peoples of the globe. [2]

"You dance with the girl with whom you came," said Joseph Campbell. And, as in marriage, you know that there are others you could marry, or could have, but that your character and your identity are bound up in making a commitment to one whom you will love with all your heart and soul and mind and strength, without averting your eyes. And maybe that's something of what Jesus meant when he said that no one comes to the Father except through him, that at some point you have to make a commitment if you are to know true fulfillment in life. And that your way, your truth, and your life are found there.

Chapter Seven

God's Wrath

Judgment and grace are inseparable theological categories. Grace without judgment is not just, and judgment without grace knows no mercy. One of the great human fears for people of faith is that God is not as loving and forgiving as we hope, but rather is keeping a tally card on all our sins and transgressions, eagerly awaiting the opportunity to ring down fire and brimstone on otherwise kindly mortals.

Is God a God of wrath or a God of forgiveness, and can we even speak of God's nature in such an arbitrary way? The witness of the Bible is multifaceted and complex. Some contemporary writers and theologians believe that God's identity develops and changes in the Bible. Whether it is actually our human understanding of God that changes or God's own self that changes is unclear. In Genesis, for instance, scholars say God grows in self-understanding through experience with the Creation and with humanity. As noted in the sermon that follows, Walter Brueggemann says God learns, repents, changes, grieves, and rejoices in the book of Genesis.

The Flood story shows us a God who does a terrible thing—floods the earth, destroying all living things except those who have been chosen to survive, Noah and his family, and Noah's selection of two living creatures of all the species on earth. It is a frightening story if taken at face value, a story that is often recounted in children's stories and Sunday school lessons. Such a familiar story usually loses its shock value after we have read it to our children as a bedtime story; but read as a text for preaching, it offers a teachable opportunity to dig deeper into the images of God we hold in our minds and hearts. Looking at it closely helps us understand how humble we must be when trying to speak of the nature of God.

My own experience in writing this sermon was one of changed perspective, mirroring the development in the story itself. I found I moved from anger and rejection of the idea of a destructive God judging and condemning the earth, to a new understanding of a God who repents and takes compassion on humanity, realizing that the flood was pitiless and tragic for all, including God.

The Flood

Genesis 6–8; Isaiah 41:4b-10 FEW STORIES IN THE BIBLE ARE AS well known as is the story of Noah and the Flood. It is memorable because of its characters and events—the ark, the animals entering two by two, the waters rising, the imagined incredulity of Noah's neighbors watching him build a strange-looking boat in his driveway, and the later picture of the earth consumed by water. I am not sure why it is so appealing to us, except perhaps that we have romanticized the picture of all the creatures lining up to get on the boat, a floating zoo. Or maybe we identify with Noah and think of ourselves as the kind of folks who would be saved if there were a worldwide flood. Or perhaps we are captivated by the mystery of whether or not the remnants of an ark might ever be found on Mt. Ararat and therefore confirm at least something in our faith. So, comedian Bill Cosby pokes fun at it, and children's toy manufacturers have had a heyday fabricating miniature arks with tiny animals and secret compartments.

And books. There are countless children's books about the Flood. One I know starts with a poem by Jacobus Revius, a seventeenth-century Dutch poet:

High and long,
Thick and strong,
Wide and stark,
Was the Ark.
Climb on board,
Said the Lord.
Noah's kin,
clambered in.
Cow and moose,
hare and goose,

> Sheep and fox,
> bee and ox. [1]

For several lines the cuteness of the story is expressed, and toward the end of the poem the tragedy:

> But the rest,
> worst and best,
> stayed on shore,
> were no more.
> That whole host,
> gave the ghost.
> They were killed,
> for the guilt,
> Which brought all,
> to the Fall.

This last part makes the point. The Flood is not a children's story at all, but rather a heavy theological treatise of grave import. And if you think about it, you might wonder why in the world we think of this as a children's story at all. Most children, if they truly hear the story, ought to have nightmares about the events reported in the sixth through the eighth chapters of Genesis.

> *The Flood is not a children's story at all, but rather a heavy theological treatise of grave import.*

At least at surface level, the story we think we know is the story of a human race that is exceedingly disobedient. We see it through the first chapters in Genesis. Betrayal in the garden of Eden. Lies. Murder. Not a pretty sight. God decides to start over again, wash away all the earth in a gigantic flood. One family, that of Noah, a righteous man who walked with God, is chosen to be saved; that family, and two of every species of animal Noah could find, one male and one female. The day comes; the thunderclouds start rolling in, and the rains begin to beat down. It rains for forty days and forty nights. The entire earth is flooded, and every living thing is destroyed, save the creatures enduring the waves in the tossing ark.

When the torrents are over and the waters subside, Noah and the animals leave the ark; God makes a new covenant with Noah, his descendants, and all the creatures of the earth, that never again shall God destroy the earth with a flood. God and the Creation shall henceforth enter into a new relationship, and the rainbow shall be a reminder to God of that understanding.

> *At one level the story appears to be the account of a vindictive and angry God who wakes up one morning, has regular instead of decaf, throws a fit, and decides, like some frenzied sculptor, to take a hammer to Creation and start all over again.*

At one level the story appears to be the account of a vindictive and angry God who wakes up one morning, has regular instead of decaf, throws a fit, and decides, like some frenzied sculptor, to take a hammer to Creation and start all over again.

I don't know what it does for you, but it doesn't do much to encourage me. The God who brings floods and wipes out the Creation is a God I have difficulty liking. And I am not the only one. This is, after all, the fulfillment of our greatest fear, that God is angry, fearful, and terrible. And yet no one I know has ever suggested that the Flood story is too strong or depicts a God we cannot love and worship. So why has this story remained in the canon of biblical literature, and is there something in it that is broader and better than its apparent image of an angry God who solves problems with temper tantrums?

Let's score a couple of points for clarity at the outset. Anyone who has taken a Bible-as-literature course in college knows that flood stories were common in the ancient world. The Gilgamesh epic and other mythological stories of floods abound in ancient cultures. But the fact that the Flood story of Genesis is not unique does not disprove its ability to bear truth. Neither should we assume that this is the ancient Hebrew adaptation of the story of another culture. After all, neither uniqueness nor similarity to other stories ever necessarily proves anything about the truth a story bears.

Second, the story is not a myth; it is a story of faith, with a point to make that is not scientific in nature but theological in impact and import.

And finally, let's be clear that while the story is filled with memorable events—the flood, the devastation of humanity, the rainbow sign, all of which grab our attention and carry our sympathies—the real import of the story is not to be found in any of these. Because it's not a folk legend of where the rainbow came from, or why there was once a great flood on earth. No, the real heart of this story can only be discovered if we look not at the water, nor the rainbow, nor even the loss of life. What we must look for in this Flood account is the story within the story, the one that takes us deep into the heart and mind of God, lays bare God's feelings, and then leaves us with a hope and a promise.

In order to hear that story, you and I will have to suspend our usual understandings of God. We must question our basic

What we must look for in this Flood account is the story within the story, the one that takes us deep into the heart and mind of God, lays bare God's feelings, and then leaves us with a hope and a promise.

assumption that God is the same yesterday, today, and forever, that God is unchangeable and cannot be swayed by what God sees. For the God of the Flood story is a God who changes.

The earliest understandings of God found in the Scriptures recounts God as a God of compassion and feeling. Those earliest writers saw Yahweh in unabashedly human terms, wracked by heartbreak, torn by disappointment, sorrowful and melancholy, grief-stricken, and feeling betrayed. Most of the time most of us think of God as immutable, impassive, and unfeeling, the God who set the laws and orders of the universe in place and then stepped back and let things unwind without further intervention.

In contrast, God, in the sixth chapter of Genesis, looks at the world and sees that things are not going well. The first man and woman have abandoned the freedom and beauty of the garden, becoming too smart for their own non-existent britches, eating of the tree of the knowledge of good and evil. There is fratricide in the family, and things go downhill from there. God sees that the wickedness of the earth and of humankind is great, and according to the writer of this part of Genesis, "The LORD was sorry that he had made humankind on the earth, and it grieved him to his heart" (Gen. 6:6).

God is not angered, but *grieved*; not enraged, but *saddened*.[2] From this point on, the primary actor and center of attention in the story is not who we thought it was—not Noah, not humanity, not the Creation, not even the flood itself, for all are secondary to the primary actor, who is God. It is not a story to explain an ancient flood and why it happened. It is not cosmology, but biography. It is the story of a God whose mind changes and who enters into the pain of

It is not a story to explain an ancient flood and why it happened. It is not cosmology, but biography.

the human condition, suffers in that pain, acts and then repents, and finally promises never to forsake the Creation again. But I get ahead of myself.

The story of Noah and the Flood addresses the question of how God will deal with a world in rebellion. How will God deal with us even when we are disobedient and destructive?

The story has two indivisible movements. The first is the flood. God's disappointment with the earth causes God to be sorry that the world is at all. So God sends a flood to blot out this veil of tears. Every living thing is destroyed. A new Creation is left in its wake. It is devastating, yes. Nearly impossible to fathom. All the earth blotted out in forty days in a flood that no sandbagging can prevent. It is horrible to imagine. But that is only half the story, which is where the redeeming social and theological value comes in.

There is one who is righteous, who walks with the Lord. He is saved; he, his family, and enough of the species of animals and birds and everything that creeps on the earth, so as to make a fresh start when the waters recede. So, after the flood, God provides for life to go on, life taken from the old order. Thus, God has compassion on Noah and on the motley crew on board the ark. And to Noah's credit, when the flood is over, he offers up a fragrant sacrifice of burnt offerings, which turn God's heart in pity towards Noah. And God remembers him, which is to say God has compassion on him. And in that compassion God, like a parent who sees the helplessness of her child, is moved in heart with sadness and swears never to do such a terrible thing again.

Nothing has happened in the story to cause this change of heart except the offering of thanksgiving Noah offers. Nothing in the flood has changed anything, not the loss of life, nor any sign of repentance; nothing in the animals or the creatures or the trees or in anything on earth. The only thing that changes is the heart of God, who decides that from this time forth and forevermore the Creation will be treated to unlimited patience and forbearance. It is not because humanity moves toward God that the crisis is resolved; it is because God moves toward humanity.

This happens because God decides two things: The first is that humanity is hopeless; the Creation will not change because it is deeply set against God's purposes. All the terrors of the waters have not changed that. And if that were not already clear from our experience, it will become abundantly clear in the next chapter of the story, as Noah goes from the altar to the wine press, gets drunk, and lays naked in his tent, to the shame of his sons. And so the new Adam, Noah, is not any better as a human being than was his great-great-grandfather, Adam of the famous Fall. God sees in all the Creation, even in Noah, that humanity is hopeless.

> *It is not because humanity moves toward God that the crisis is resolved; it is because God moves toward humanity.*

The second thing God decides is that God will not be dissuaded from the divine dream for the earth and its people, in spite of their rebellion. Even though humanity is hopeless, God will not give up hope in us. No more floods, ever, as a sign of God's displeasure; from now on, only patience.

There is movement in this story. At the beginning we see a God who is heartbroken at the fall of humanity and who brings a costly judgment against the earth; guilt leads to punishment. But at the end of the story we see a God whose heart has changed and who resolves never to break a new covenant of kindliness and patience toward the earth, toward all of us. So Walter Brueggemann writes:

> There may be death and destruction. [And] evil has not been eradicated from creation. But we are now assured that these

are not rooted in the anger or rejection of God. The relation of creator to creature is no longer in a scheme of retribution. Because of a revolution in the heart of God, that relation is now based in unqualified grace. [3]

So much for the idea that the God of the Old Testament is a God of anger and judgment, and the God of the New Testament a God of grace and forgiveness. For here in the Flood story we see God learning through grief, that judgment without mercy is futile.

The same love for the Creation that caused God to make a new covenant with Noah is echoed again and again elsewhere in the Scriptures. It is the love for Israel expressed in Isaiah's description of God's words to Israel, "I have chosen you and not cast you off; . . . do not be afraid, for I am your God" (Isa. 41:9-10).

God's amazing love for us, learned through the hard lessons of disappointment and sorrow, is that even though we are not deserving, even though God knows we will fail at returning God's love, even though we are thoroughly human and fall far short of God's grace, God loves us still.

It is the love God expresses for us all in giving us Jesus Christ. As Paul says, "At the right time Christ died for the ungodly. . . . [And] God proves his love for us in that while we still were sinners Christ died for us" (Rom. 5:6, 8).

God's amazing love for us, learned through the hard lessons of disappointment and sorrow, is that even though we are not deserving, even though God knows we will fail at returning God's love, even though we are thoroughly human and fall far short of God's grace, God loves us still.

This is, of course, the lesson of love that parents learn (though some parents never do), that you love your children simply because they are yours. And while they may disappoint you, fall short of what is best for them, and even disobey you and defy you willfully, they are yours, bone of your bone and flesh of your flesh, and you cannot stop loving them. You can never stop loving them; it's just not in you.

We do not love, any of us, because the one we love has earned that love or deserves it. Love just doesn't work that way. We love because they *are*, and because we need to love, and need to be loved. It's as simple and as complicated as that. Which is, of course, why God's love for us is so simple and yet so complicated. God loves us simply because we are, because God needs to love us, would not be complete without loving us.

Waters receded, back to dry land, all the debris cleared away—I'm still not sure that I like the story of the Flood very much. It appears so cruel at surface level. All the world swept away under water. I think I could do without it. I *think* I could.

What I cannot do without is that God who has promised never to forsake or leave me, come hell or high water. That God who has promised to set the rainbow in the sky as a sign of an everlasting covenant, and who tells me, "Do not fear, I am with you." It is that God who finally emerges from the story of the Flood and whose love is from everlasting to everlasting. I may not want to have anything to do with that story of the Flood, but I cannot do without its God who promises that

> When through the deep waters I call you to go,
> The rivers of sorrow shall not overflow,
> For I will be with you in trouble to bless
> And sanctify to you your deepest distress.[4]

To that God be all glory, all praise, and thanksgiving. To that God may the pleasing odors of our burnt offerings ever be raised. World without end. Amen.

Chapter Eight

The Problem of God's Generosity

*The parable of the laborers in the vineyard in Matthew 20 and
the parable of the unjust steward in Luke 16 are two of the most
troubling parables Jesus ever told. Both offer nearly insoluble
problems for us when we try to unlock their mysteries with the key
of our expectations of what we think God should be and do. In the
end, both parables give us fresh insights into a God we realize we
barely know.*

*In the parable of the laborers, a naive reading of the passage
tells us that something is wrong here. Everyone is being paid the
same wage regardless of how long or how hard they have worked.
There is no justice in this parable, especially when seen from an
allegorical perspective in which God is likened to the vineyard
owner, we are the diligent and faithful laborers hired for the
longest time, and those who come on the scene last, work the least,
loaf the most, and don't carry their weight are paid the same
wages of eternal life.*

*The theological issue at stake is salvation by grace, and the
problem we all have in giving up the idea that we can earn our
way into heaven. It is one thing to give lip service to our belief
that God is God and we are not, and that God can do whatever
God chooses to show divine grace; it is quite another to hear Jesus
tell a story illustrating this point in earthly terms that angers and
confuses us because of its paucity of justice and abundance of grace.
Even I had to realize and accept that I, too, have much at stake
that comes under attack in this parable. If all the hours of weekend
weddings, the midnight calls to the emergency room, the sixty-
hour work weeks, the theological degrees, and community service*

*do not add up in my favor in some heavenly column, then what do
I have to show for all that I have done for the commonwealth of
God? Is a slap on the back and a hearty "Well done, thou good and
faithful servant" really enough?*

*The parable breaks open our understanding of any notions we
might have had that the justice of heaven in which there are ironclad rules of rewards and punishments may not be all that we have
expected. I like Grant Gilmore's description of how grace and justice interrelate in heavenly places.*

> *The better the society, the less law there will be. In Heaven there
> will be no law, and the lion will lie down with the lamb. The val-
> ues of an unjust society will reflect themselves in an unjust law.
> The worse the society, the more law there will be. In hell there will
> be nothing but law, and due process will be meticulously observed.[1]*

*Ironically, there is no problem internal to the text in this para-
ble. The problem is in our hearing of it. We want to hear this
parable as a text about divine justice, but instead it is a parable
about mercy and grace. The challenge for the preacher is to rein-
terpret the parable in such a way as to help both preacher and congregation understand that our point of view will determine
whether or not we can hear the grace inherent in the text or
merely be angered by its apparent injustice.*

The Evil Eye

Matthew 20:1-16

OUR SUPERSTITIONS SAY A GREAT deal about us. Spill salt and throw some over your shoulder to break the spell. Shatter a mirror and it sends a shiver down your back for fear of the next seven years. A black cat crosses the path ahead and you look to see if there's another way to pass. Even though you may not be superstitious, encounter these and you still remember the superstition.

It is no different in the Middle East. One of the most prevalent of Middle Eastern superstitions is that associated with the evil eye. Last year on a trip to Israel, I learned about that tradition and how to ward off its power. As you wander about the bazaars in the Old City of Jerusalem, you'll see huge bins of souvenir evil eyes, agate-like charms meant to ward off certain powers. And like rabbit's feet in our culture, the tradition that surrounds the superstition for many people is ingrained.

It's hard to know where this superstition got its start, but one thing is for sure, it is ancient. It was known to Jesus. The Greek original is a figure of speech translated "the evil in your eye," and it is used as an expression meaning "envy." The amulets and trinkets sold in the bazaars are meant to ward off the power of envy, the discontent you feel when another has an advantage or something you want.

It figures in the parable of the laborers in the vineyard, in Matthew 20, which might also be described as the parable of the generous vintner. In fact it is the evil eye that unlocks the meaning of the parable.

The way Jesus told it, there was a vineyard owner who was short on day laborers; so the owner went to the hiring hall and found some people at daybreak who would sign on

for a day's work at a day's wages, one denarius. So the laborers, glad to have the work, gathered up their pruning snips
and sunscreen and went out into the fields to do an honest
day's work.

> *The way Jesus told it, there was a vineyard owner*
> *who was short on day laborers and so he went to the*
> *hiring hall and found some people at daybreak who*
> *would sign on for a day's work at a day's wages, one*
> *denarius.*

There was planting and pruning and picking to be done.
And if they were transplanting, having looked at the coun-
tryside around Jerusalem and in Galilee, there is no question that there would be lots of rock tilling and
transporting, taking the rocks and boulders, which are
everywhere in the earth, to the borders of the vineyard both
to mark the boundary and to get them out of the way. It
must have been hard work, tiring and sweaty.

While the first batch of workers hired at daybreak were
toiling away, the vineyard owner decided that he could use
some more people in the field. So about nine o'clock in the
morning he drove his pickup truck back over to the hiring
hall, told the folks that were standing around that if they
wanted to work he'd pay them rightly. They hopped in the
back of the truck and went to work in the field.

By then the heat of the day was starting to show. And by
noon the temperature was up around ninety. They had
some fruit and pita bread and some water at the lunch
break, but since the day was partly gone and there was still a
lot to do, and many hands make light work, the vineyard
owner went out again to see if he could scour up some more
workers. He did, and they came to work in the field. At
three in the afternoon, still more workers were hired. And

last but not least, a couple of hours before evening, as quitting time drew near, the vineyard owner found a few stray folks leaning over the fence of the vineyard without anything to do, watching the others work. And he said, "Come on in, get to work, and I'll pay you for what you do." So they came in and worked the cleanup shift.

Word traveled fast down the line that the vineyard owner was more generous than the workers had ever expected, because those who were hired just before the end of the day were getting a denarius.

As the sun was setting, everybody who had labored in the vineyard that day gathered in groups and lined up according to the number of hours they had worked, from the last hired to the first. As the landowner started to hand out the checks, those who were hired last and had worked the least amount of time were paid a denarius, a full day's wage.

Word traveled fast down the line that the vineyard owner was more generous than the workers had ever expected, because those who were hired just before the end of the day were getting a denarius. The ones who were at the end of the line were thrilled. They all began to elbow one another and joke around and think about what they were going to do with the bonuses they were anticipating. They had the math all worked out: "If five'll getcha ten, ten'll getcha twenty." Some were thinking about back-to-school shoes for the kids. Others could see a bottle of nice wine for dinner that night and a thick filet mignon. Still others were thinking about making an extra dent in their credit card payment for the month. And all of them were thinking what a great guy the owner of the vineyard was. In fact, they started to sing "For He's a Jolly Good Fellow."

But then, the vineyard owner moved down the line to the

workers who were hired at three o'clock, and for their efforts, he paid out the same, one denarius, the wage that was paid to the johnny-come-latelys hired at five. The singing stopped and word started to spread down the line that something was amiss.

When the workers hired at noon were paid a denarius, followed by the same to the nine o'clock hands, and finally the daybreak crowd, the vineyard owner was facing the swelling anger of an irate mob. The workers hired at sunset felt exhilarated and the daybreak employees felt swindled because everybody was paid the same regardless of how long or how hard they had worked.

One of the all-day workers was elected union steward and pushed to the fore by the others to speak for them all. He grumbled about the inequity of the pay. But the landowner said that those hired first were paid in full, according to the contract; they got what they agreed upon. And did they begrudge the landowner doing whatever he wanted with what was his? Or, in precisely Jesus' words, "Do you have the evil eye?" The vineyard owner asked, "Do you envy the last hired because they have the good fortune to receive my generosity?" What a good question!

We might wonder about that vineyard and its labor practices, whether anyone showed up for work at daybreak the next day. But then, what is described in this parable has nothing to do with fairness; it has only to do with grace, and grace seems a lot more gracious if you only have to work an hour to get a lot more than you deserve.

The eye of almost all of us goes with the laborers who worked the longest. We feel anger and frustration for them

What is described in this parable has nothing to do with fairness; it has only to do with grace, and grace seems a lot more gracious if you only have to work an hour to get a lot more than you deserve.

that they are not paid a big bonus for bearing the heat of the day and the exhaustion of working the longest hours. It must be something like what the ballplayer who signed a five-year contract for $75,000 a year feels when he bats .429 and is voted the league's most valuable player, while a rookie who signed on for a million and a half for five years shows up for spring training ten pounds overweight and ends up batting .203 for the season. There's just no justice in it.

This parable is not a justification for unfair labor practices, although it may be fodder for the appropriateness of affirmative action. But to spend too much time thinking about the poor old workers who worked so hard and were gypped by the vineyard owner is to miss the larger issue that's present here, the issue of heaven's justice, which is really grace. For that's how Jesus introduces the parable at its outset: "The kingdom of heaven is like a landowner who went out early in the morning to hire laborers."

You need to know that just before Jesus tells the parable, Peter tells Jesus that he and the other disciples have risked everything to follow him. Jesus assures him that everyone who has left home and family and livelihood for his sake will receive a hundredfold in return, and eternal life.

What follows the parable is the teaching of Jesus that he would be going up to Jerusalem, be handed over to the chief priests, condemned to death, and crucified. That's followed by the story of James and John's mother coming to Jesus and asking for special favors in heaven, for her boys to sit at his right and his left in glory.

Jesus is the only one in this section of the Gospel who seems to understand that the price of discipleship is not a

Jesus is the only one in this section of the Gospel who seems to understand that the price of discipleship is not a matter of rewards, but of sacrifice.

matter of rewards, but of sacrifice. After all, he would be going to Jerusalem to die. In the meantime the disciples were trying to figure out how much good stuff was in it for them. Like the laborers who started at daybreak, they saw Jesus doing good things—healing, forgiving sins, giving people hope; so they must have thought that in heaven— since they had labored so long and were in the inner circle and all—they could expect extra blessings and preferential treatment. But in this parable Jesus teaches them, and us, that God's grace is preposterously and aggravatingly generous to everyone.

From the point of view of justice, there is a case to be made against God, who in this case is more gracious than just: too kind, too much of a pushover, too softhearted and liberal in passing out the goodness and mercy of heaven.

It grates against the way we like things to work, which is solid, businesslike principles: "You pay for what you get, and you get what you pay for." "An honest day's work for an honest day's wages." "The early bird gets the worm." We like God to be a fair dealer. We expect ironclad justice. We like sinners held accountable; the fires of hell kept hot for those who are evil, the murderer, the rapist, the child molester. We like the Ten Commandments because they're clear, concise, uncompromising, and you can get them on a wallet-sized card and commit them to memory. We like our God neat and tidy, clearheaded and holding the world accountable. We don't want God slobbering over others with sympathy, forgiving everything as if nothing was abhorrent or evil.

If it doesn't make any difference who you are in the heavenly places, how much credit you've racked up, and how many hours you've donated to the church and the United Way and the Junior Board and the Cancer Society, then what's the point? Why lead a life on the straight and narrow? Why work yourself to the bone for the things you believe in? Why would you drive for Meals on Wheels, or be a deacon, or take an elderly neighbor to a doctor's appointment, or volunteer at the soup kitchen, or come to worship every Sunday, or pray, or read the Bible? Why bother? If God's grace is equally generous to those who knock themselves out to do heaven's work in the same way as those who barely lift a finger for heaven's sake, then why work so hard on heaven's behalf?

If it doesn't make any difference who you are in the heavenly places, how much credit you've racked up, and how many hours you've donated to the church and the United Way and the Junior Board and the Cancer Society, then what's the point?

Well, first of all, because the whole point of being invited into the vineyard is not for benefits, but for sacrifice. Jesus put it best when, at the end of this very chapter in which the parable is told, he tells his disciples, "Whoever wishes to be great among you must be your servant . . . just as the Son of Man came not to be served but to serve, and to give his life a ransom for many." The way of discipleship is the way of service, and sometimes the rewards are delayed, and often the hours are long, and sometimes those who are in there with you are more a source of irritation and aggravation than a source of joy. But the invitation goes to whomever God chooses, not to those whom we choose.

More importantly, we work hard on heaven's behalf, serving God and one another, because of the inestimable joy of being in the vineyard in the first place. It is an invitation to be close to God. It is to be welcome in the courts of grace itself, and no reward there is inadequate.

God's nature is to lavish love on us, far more than we deserve and much more than we might have ever expected, and no one will be left out who has labored. Does that mean that God is a pushover, soft on crime, and weak on the character issue? Not at all. It simply means that God is God and we are not, and it's God's vineyard, so God can do what God wants to do. Do you have the evil eye? Are you envious because God is generous?

> *God's nature is to lavish love on us, far more than we deserve and much more than we might have ever expected, and no one will be left out who has labored.*

You do understand, don't you, that it is not God who is unjust in this parable of the laborers in the vineyard? It is those who resent the grace of God being given in such surprising measure to those whom the world deems unworthy. The evil here is not with the landowner, who may do what he wishes with what blessings he has. The evil is truly in the eye of the beholder.

Long ago Jesus told this parable of the laborers in the vineyard, and even now, centuries later, our eyes tend to fix on the justice instead of the grace, the inequity felt by those who worked the longest and received the same as those who worked the shortest. And that is because only those who were called at the latest hour and have worked the shortest time truly understand just how generous the owner is in giving them all they receive.

> *The evil here is not with the landowner, who may do what he wishes with what blessings he has. The evil is truly in the eye of the beholder.*

If the parable still bothers you, it's because you have misunderstood with whom to identify in the story. For in order to get the twist that is there you must know that we are those hired *last*, not hired *first*. Which is why now you either get the grace that is in it, or you don't.

Chapter Nine

The Value of Time

One of the most complicated and difficult parables Jesus ever told is that of the unjust steward, found in Luke 16. It defies allegorical interpretation and begs the question of the reward given the steward for his dishonest business practices. Is Jesus implying a new beatitude, "Blessed are the clever"?

We know that in the real world the unjust prosper while the good suffer. Any attempt to articulate a morality that ignores that fact is less than complete. In the book of Job we see what happens when well-intentioned and faithful people try to do this. As each of Job's friends tries to make sense of his misfortune by blaming him for his unrighteousness, their efforts provide inadequate and inappropriate answers.

In this parable, the crux of the problem comes in the summary verse 9, which advises the children of light to "make friends for yourselves by means of dishonest wealth so that when it is gone, they may welcome you into the eternal homes." What is it that we are being asked to do?

A second look at the parable suggests that the apparent reversal of morality that verse 9 holds out is not all there is to this parable. We must ask what it is that causes the steward to act so cleverly. The answer is that he discovers what time it is. It is time for an accounting of his stewardship. The master wants to know what the steward has done with that with which he has been entrusted. The movement here is from the ethical to the eschatological. The time is at hand, the books are to be closed, and the master demands an accounting from the steward.

The movement of the sermon shifts from the question of whether the clever are rewarded to the matter of whether our stewardship of life reckons with what time it is. What kind of stewards of our lives we will be is shaped decisively by whether or not we know that an accounting is imminent and inevitable.

Blessed Are the Clever?

Luke 16:1-9 DENY ALL OTHER CLAIMS ABOUT JESUS, and you still must admit that he was a marvelous storyteller. The characters who populate his stories are memorable. There is a prodigal son who takes his inheritance and strays into the world of city slickers and casino life and discovers that he misses his family. There is a good Samaritan who binds the wounds of a mugging victim and proves a friend to an enemy. There is a rich man who goes to hell because of his indifference to the poor, and a poor man named Lazarus who goes to heaven with its many mansions, one of which becomes his very own.

> *Deny all other claims about Jesus, and you still must admit that he was a marvelous storyteller.*

And then there is the parable of the unjust steward, perhaps the most puzzling and controversial story Jesus ever told because of the way it mixes apparent good with apparent bad, what seems like evil with what seems like good. In other words, it's hard to tell in this parable what is virtue and what is vice.

Let's enter into the world of the parable for a moment and see if we can figure out who is doing what to whom. Once upon a time, Jesus said, there was a rich man who had a steward, a kind of business manager, and charges were brought to the man that this steward was wasting his goods. The problem here sounds like a simple personnel issue. Malfeasance in the workplace. The steward will need to be reprimanded and let go. It's cut-and-dried.

Complications set in when the steward is allowed a few extra days to audit the books and submit a financial statement. Between Friday and Monday, when the books were due, the steward went around to all the rich man's debtors and cooked the books. He marked down a percentage of all the debt owed by each, and thereby ingratiated himself to all the people to whom he would be looking for help in his impending unemployment.

"How much do you owe my master?" he asked one.

"A hundred measures of oil."

"Take your bill quickly," he said, "and write down fifty."

"And how much do you owe?" he asked another.

"A hundred measures of wheat," came the answer.

"Hurry, take your bill and write eighty."

> *I see him sitting at a table, a bare lightbulb swinging from a single wire overhead, sleeves rolled up, sweat rolling down his neck, a green visor shading his forehead, and two sets of books splayed in front of him—like a waiter doing his taxes and trying to hide the tips.*

It's hard to tell here whether the steward was cutting out his markup, eliminating the usury charges, or just stealing from the rich man by lowering the debt. But I think it's reasonable, in light of the economy of this parable, to view the steward in the most pejorative way. I see him sitting at a table, a bare lightbulb swinging from a single wire overhead, sleeves rolled up, sweat rolling down his neck, a green visor shading his forehead, and two sets of books splayed in front of him—like a waiter doing his taxes and trying to hide the tips. Yet with each unsuspecting debtor who comes in for an accounting, he pulls another fast move and reduces the account, ingratiating himself to each. By the end of the day, he has done pretty well for himself; and the debtors have done pretty well, too. The only one who hasn't made some form of profit is the rich man, whose assets have been whittled away by the steward's feathering of his own nest.

Reason dictates that this mole should not only be fired, but turned over to the D.A. for grand larceny. And if there is any justice at all, he should be sent up the river for a long stretch to think about the consequences of being so clever. Except that, according to the parable, Monday morning when the rich man calls the steward to account and demands his key to the executive washroom, the rich man is so favorably impressed by the way the steward has used his noodle to get ahead that he commends the dishonest steward for his cleverness (the RSV calls it his "prudence"). And Jesus sums up the meaning of the parable by saying that the children of this world are wiser in their generation than the children of light. Which sounds like we good law-abiding people should take a lesson from the scoundrels. Is Jesus giving us a new beatitude, "Blessed are the clever"?

In the verses that follow the story, there are three different attempts by Luke to explain the meaning of the parable. The first says, do like the shady steward and make friends with unrighteous money so that when it fails you'll have friends in high places. The second says that you must do well with a little or you won't be entrusted with more. And the third says you can't serve God and money, so make a choice. Evidently Luke had as much trouble making sense of the parable as we do. But none of these attempts to explain the steward is very satisfying because it's nigh onto impossible to make peace with the dishonesty of the rascal who gets rewarded for his shady morality.

I have not read a commentary nor found a biblical scholar who feels on firm ground in trying to make sense of this parable. It's that ambiguous.

In a sense the storyline fits the occasional characterization that sometimes emerges in Scripture: the character of the rogue, the impish trickster who is held forth as a hero. Jacob is the best example; Jacob the trickster who pulls the wool over his father's eyes and makes off with his brother's inheritance.

But in another sense this parable is also like the one that precedes it—the parable of the prodigal son, in which a crisis causes the morally compromised protagonist to do an about-face and receive an unmerited reward. And it is also a bit like that parable in which a vineyard owner hires laborers at varying times of the day but pays them all the same at the end of the day because the boss has the infuriating right to do whatever he pleases with whomever he wants, like the landowner in this parable who rewards a scoundrel. But while there are echoes of all of these in this parable it's not exactly the same, because we're left hanging with what appears as a vice described as a virtue, Jesus telling us, "Make friends for yourselves by means of dishonest wealth so that when it is gone, they may welcome you into the eternal homes."

As we hear this parable we must not overlook two important elements that may help us unlock its mystery. One is the issue of time. Time is emphasized by the fact that the accounts have come due and the steward has only a brief time to get things moving in his favor, a fact that's underscored when he tells the debtors to change their account balances *quickly* (Luke 16:6).

And the second is the comedy in the parable, the laughable nature of what is happening, so extreme that it is

Imagine the scene in which the steward stands before his boss and the rich man opens the ledger to see just how bad things are; it's so bad that all the landowner can do is roar with laughter and commend the steward on his cleverness.

absurd. If you think about it, the forgiveness of the rich landowner is preposterous. Imagine the scene in which the steward stands before his boss and the rich man opens the ledger to see just how bad things are; it's so bad that all the landowner can do is roar with laughter and commend the steward on his cleverness. This is the most unlikely thing that can happen, and so it is laughable. Either there is laughter or there is murder, and since murder is not reported, there must have been laughter.

We do know there was laughter in the room where Jesus told the parable, because the scene immediately shifts to the Pharisees, whom we are told loved money and that they laughed at Jesus' story; in fact they ridiculed Jesus for his story. To them it sounded like a joke. It sounded like, "Have you heard the one about the crooked accountant who was stealing money from his boss, and when the boss found out and asked him to account for the losses, the accountant went out and stole some more. And then, because he was so clever, the boss gave him a bonus." The moral order of a just and lawful society is ridiculed by the outcome of this parable. And the Pharisees heard that and thought it must be a joke.

They loved money, these Pharisees. They were in the business of collecting fees for sacrifices, raking off a bit of the take on the pigeon sales and cereal commodities. Money was serious business to them. So they didn't want to take it seriously. They ridiculed Jesus for it. It was absurd.

> *Think of this parable as a shell game. Keep your eye on the pea under the shell.*

And at last the fog starts to lift and the parable starts to make sense because of the reaction of the Pharisees.

Think of this parable as a shell game. Keep your eye on the pea under the shell. As the shells are moved on the table, we think we have the answer, until at last the shell where we think the pea is lodged is lifted and we see that it is not where the pea is located at all.

You see, the point of the parable is that it's not a story about money. That's just a distraction. Our eyes, like the eyes of the Pharisees, go with the money, with the cleverness of the steward who is able to get something for nothing by going around and making deals for himself. We're entranced by the cleverness of the steward because we're more interested in the money than we are anything else.

The bedrock issue in this parable is that of time and the stewardship of our gifts, the realization that we have been wasting the master's goods and, worse yet, soon we will be called to account for it.

But money and cleverness are not the ultimate issues here, any more than wasting money is the issue in the parable that precedes it, the parable of the prodigal son. The bedrock issue in this parable is that of time and the stewardship of our gifts, the realization that we have been wasting the master's goods and, worse yet, soon we will be called to account for it.

For all the bad that the dishonest steward does, he has one redeeming quality: he has a sense of how much time he has, and he does what he can to redeem his situation in the time that is available. Therein lies a truth. If you were to take a random sample of people as to what are the most valuable things they have, they would likely list their possessions—a house, a car, some investments; in a word, things of financial worth. Some would probably say their children, or their spouse, or their work. But what the steward in the parable makes plain in his frenzied struggle to better his future is that none of these is the most valuable commodity on earth.

Time is. Time is all the steward has to work out his salvation, low-sighted as that salvation may be. And he does a remarkable job of it. He summons what assets he has and makes friends in the world so that when cast into it penniless he may have a place to go and friends to take pity on him.

What the steward realizes is that he does not have forever, that the accounts are being called in, and he must show what he's done. While he's not a paragon of virtue in the way he goes about it, he cannot be faulted for his awareness of the immediacy of his situation. He knows what time it is because his illusion that he has forever has been shattered.

> *We sign for the five-year payment plan on the new $30,000 sport utility vehicle and are more stunned by the sticker price than by the brass we are exhibiting in imagining that it is certain we will be around or even employed to make all the payments.*

This is not an easy truth for us to hear, since most of us are banking on tomorrow, and we bank on it because the uncertainty of tomorrow escapes us. We take out the thirty-year mortgage on the house and barely blink. We sign for the five-year payment plan on the new $30,000 sport utility vehicle and are more stunned by the sticker price than by the brass we are exhibiting in imagining that it is certain we will be around or even employed to make all the payments. Without our realizing it, we have fallen for the illusion of immortality.

The late Henri Nouwen, the Dutch priest and theologian, writes about this illusion of immortality that we all have. He says, "Although we have learned . . . that we are worth more than what the world makes us, we keep giving an eternal value to the things we own, the people we all know, the plans we have, and the successes we 'collect.'"[1] And he's right.

We are like the steward before the fall, thinking we have forever to accumulate our wealth and save for our future, but his future came home to roost suddenly and then he had nothing at all.

Each fall, like most pastors, I preach about stewardship, and of course my congregation's eyes go glassy because they're afraid the church will somehow reach into their pockets when they're not looking and take more than they're ready to give. We think of stewardship in terms of the money we give to the church. But stewardship is far more radical, far more fundamental than the pledge we make to the church, or the gifts we drop in the plate on Sunday morning. Stewardship is what we do with what we have with our most important possessions, and no possession we have is more valuable than time.

Our illusion of immortality tells us to get comfortable and bank on tomorrow, but wisdom suggests that we make friends in heavenly places so that when the accounts are called in we have somewhere to take refuge.

Stewardship begins with knowing what time it is, and knowing also that the accounts will be called in for review. We have been given life and health and the leisure to use our lives for whatever purposes we choose, for good or for ill. Our illusion of immortality tells us to get comfortable and bank on tomorrow, but wisdom suggests that we make friends in heavenly places so that when the accounts are called in we have somewhere to take refuge. And how do you do that?

Fred Craddock points us in one direction. He writes:

Most of us will not this week christen a ship, write a book, end a war, appoint a cabinet, dine with the queen, convert a nation, or be burned at the stake. More likely the week will present no more than a chance to give a cup of water, write a note, visit a nursing home, vote for a county commissioner, teach a Sunday school class, share a meal, tell a child a story, go to choir practice, and feed the neighbor's cat. "Whoever is faithful in a very little is faithful also in much" (Luke 16:10).[2]

In other words, you prepare for the hour of accounting not by grand and glorious deeds necessarily, but by simply living a life reflecting Jesus' life, committed to him, studying his Word, showing his love, being his faithful disciple.

The parable of the dishonest steward remains one of the most confusing and convoluted parables Jesus ever told. It is a parable with several shells moving on the table all at once. And it's hard to tell where things are going. I'm not completely sure why he told it, but I do know that no one has ever had a better sense of time than he did, no better awareness that one life can do so much for good or for ill, and that we don't have forever to do it. For him time was always too short, and when the time came for him to die, it was too soon.

Is it any different for us? The accounts are always called in too soon.

Once upon a time a rich man had a steward, and word came to him that the steward was wasting his goods. So the word went out that there would be an accounting. The question is, fellow steward, what by your wit, considering the hour, will you do now?

Notes

Chapter 1. Divorce

1. Phillip Sigal, *The Halakah of Jesus of Nazareth According to the Gospel of Matthew* (Lanham, Md.: University Press of America, 1986), pp. 83-118.
2. Michael Lindvall, "Sherry Moves Home for a While," in *The Good News from North Haven* (New York: Doubleday, 1991), pp. 108-9.

Chapter 4. Homosexuality

1. William Sloane Coffin, sermon entitled "Homosexuality," printed privately by the Riverside Church in the City of New York, 420 Riverside Drive, New York, N.Y. Sermon delivered at Riverside Church on July 12, 1981.
2. See Genesis 19, Lev. 18:22, Deut. 23:17-18, Rom. 1:26-28, 1 Tim. 1:9-10, and possibly 1 Cor. 6:9.
3. For example, Lev. 25:44, Eph. 6:5, and Col. 3:22.

Chapter 6. Universalism

1. Dennis Overbye, "Who's Afraid of the Big Bad Bang?" *Time*, 26 April 1993, p. 74.
2. Gerard Sloyan, *John*, in the *Interpretation: A Bible Commentary for Preaching and Teaching Series* (Atlanta: John Knox, 1988), pp. 179-80.

Chapter 7. God's Wrath

1. Jacobus Revius, "The Great Flood." Translated by Peter Spier in *Noah's Ark* (Garden City: Doubleday & Co., 1977), p. 7.
2. This description is that of Walter Brueggemann, in his commentary *Genesis*, in *Interpretation* series (Atlanta: John Knox Press, 1982), p. 77.
3. Ibid., p. 84.
4. "How Firm a Foundation," hymn. *Rejoice in the Lord* (Grand Rapids: Eerdmans, 1985), 172.

Chapter 8. The Problem of God's Generosity

1. Grant Gilmore, *The Ages of American Law (Storrs Lectures on Jurisprudence; 1974)* (New Haven: Yale University Press, 1977), p. 111.

Chapter 9. The Value of Time

1. Henri Nouwen, *Reaching Out: The Three Movements of the Spiritual Life* (New York: Doubleday, 1975), p. 82.
2. Fred Craddock, *Luke*, in *Interpretation* series (Louisville: John Knox Press, 1990), p. 192.